Pelican Books
Alexander the Great and the Middle East

Andrew Robert Burn was born in Shropshire in 1902. He was educated at Uppingham and Christ Church, Oxford, where he took a First in Greats. His enthusiasm for Greece dates from earliest childhood, and while still an under-graduate he won the Charles Oldham Prize with an essay on the early Greek lyric poets.

During the war he was the British Council's Representative in Greece, 1940–1. He then served in the Intelligence Corps, and from 1944 to 1946 was Second Secretary in the British Embassy in Athens. His former outdoor interests include mountaineering and gliding, and he is still an enthusiastic traveller in the remoter parts of Greece and the Aegean. His books include *The World of Hesiod*, *The Lyric Age of Greece*, *The Pelican History of Greece*, and *Persia and the Greeks*, subtitled *The Defence of the West*; also *The Modern Greeks*, which he wrote in the intervals of duty at G.H.Q., Middle East, in 1941–2.

Mr Burn was Reader in Ancient History at Glasgow from 1965 to 1969, and then, until 1972 Visiting Professor at 'A College Year in Athens'.

He is married and lives in Oxfordshire.

Alexander the Great and the Middle East

A. R. Burn

Penguin Books

Penguin Books Ltd, Harmondsworth,
Middlesex, England
Penguin Books Australia Ltd, Ringwood,
Victoria, Australia

First published in the 'Teach Yourself History'
series by The English Universities Press 1947
Second edition published in Great Britain 1964
Revised edition published in Pelican Books 1973

Made and Printed in Great Britain by
Hazell Watson & Viney Ltd,
Aylesbury, Bucks
Set in Linotype Pilgrim

A General Introduction
to the 'Teach Yourself History'
Series

This series has been undertaken in the conviction that there can be no subject of study more important than history. Great as have been the conquests of natural science in our time – such that many think of ours as a scientific age *par excellence* – it is even more urgent and necessary that advances should be made in the social sciences, if we are to gain control of the forces of nature loosed upon us. The bed out of which all the social sciences spring is history; there they find, in greater or lesser degree, subject-matter and material, verification or contradiction.

There is no end to what we can learn from history, if only we will, for it is co-terminous with life. Its special field is the life of man in society, and at every point we can learn vicariously from the experience of others before us in history.

To take one point only – the understanding of politics : how can we hope to understand the world of affairs around us if we do not know how it came to be what it is? How to understand Germany, or Soviet Russia, or the United States – or ourselves, without knowing something of their history?

There is no subject that is more useful, or indeed indispensable.

Some evidence of the growing awareness of this may be seen in the immense increase in the interest of the reading public in history, and the much larger place the subject has come to take in education in our time.

This series has been planned to meet the needs and demands of a very wide public and of education – they are indeed the same. I am convinced that the most congenial, as well as the most concrete and practical, approach to history is the biographical, through the lives of the great men whose actions have been so much part of history, and whose careers in turn have been so moulded and formed by events.

The key idea of this series, and what distinguishes it from any other that has appeared, is the intention by way of a biography of a great man to open up a significant historical theme; for example, Cromwell and the Puritan Revolution, or Lenin and the Russian Revolution.

My hope is, in the end, as the series fills out and completes itself, by a sufficient number of biographies to cover whole periods and subjects in that way. To give you the history of the United States, for example, or the British Empire or France, via a number of biographies of their leading historical figures.

That should be something new, as well as convenient and practical, in education.

I need hardly say that I am a strong believer in people with good academic standards writing once more for the general reading public, and of the public being given the best that the universities can provide. From this point of view this series is intended to bring the university into the homes of the people.

A. L. Rowse
All Souls College, Oxford

To the Memory of
CHRISTOPHER BUCKLEY
who died of wounds in Korea
the 12th August, 1950,
and of his friendship, especially
in Greece and the Middle East,
1940–1943
this book is now dedicated
as formerly to him living

Contents

10 Contents

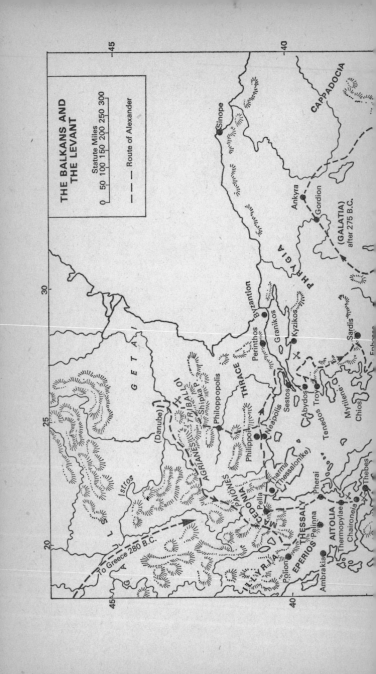

THE BALKANS AND
THE LEVANT

Statute Miles
0 50 100 150 200 250 300

— — — Route of Alexander

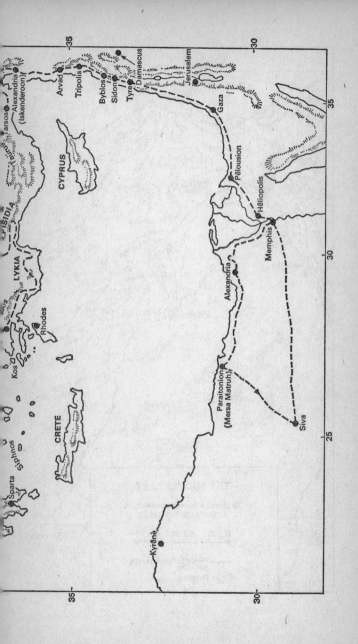

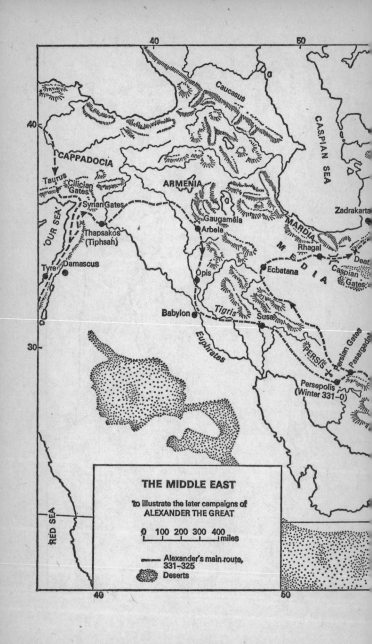

THE MIDDLE EAST

to illustrate the later campaigns of
ALEXANDER THE GREAT

0 100 200 300 400
              miles

——— Alexander's main route,
      331–325

⣿⣿⣿ Deserts

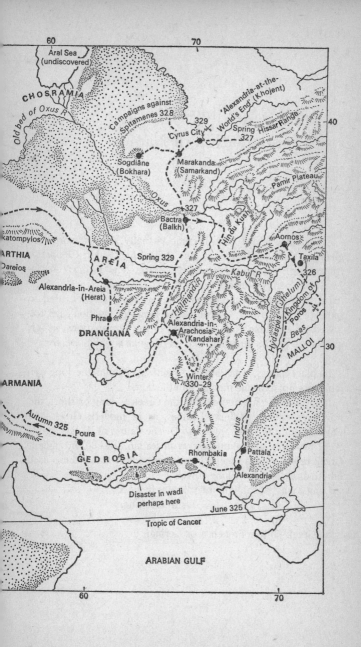

Note: Spelling and Pronunciation of Names

Names which have become virtually English words are given in their English form (e.g. Philip, Alexander, Cleopatra, Byzantium); others in their Greek form (e.g. Koinos, Meleagros, not Coenus, Meleager, etc.).

In the latter case the circumflex (∧) sign has been used to indicate long vowels, except where long 'by position', i.e. followed by a double consonant, and in the terminations, -e, -er, -or, -on (in personal names), and -es (singular), which are always long.

In place-names, e.g. Phôkis, Arachôsia, Pêlion, the long syllables are not as a rule indicated in the text.

It should be remembered that the Greek E, long or short, did not have entirely different values, as in modern Greek and English; and the same applies to O. The values of A, E, I and O were probably approximately as in Italian. 'Bê, Bê' in ancient Greek represented a sheep's bleating. And Periclean Athens used E both as a short and a long vowel.

Long â was probably more or less as in *glass*.
   „ î   „   „   „   as in *machine*.
   „ ô   „   „   „   like *-aw*.
Y (Greek U) like French u or German ü.

1 Parents and Child

(356–340 B.C.)

Olympias, Queen of Macedonia, brought forth her first-born son at Pella in the year of the 106th Olympic Games, subsequently computed by Christian historians as 356 B.C. He was a fine baby. Olympias, fierce and emotional, was passionately proud of him; no doubt she hoped that he would help to confirm her position in the affections of his father, King Philip. Philip was away, it appears, beyond Mount Olympos, taking sides in an internal war in Thessaly, and incidentally securing a foothold for certain ulterior schemes of his own. Philip received three pieces of good news that year in quick succession: that his general, Parmenion, had routed the Illyrian hill tribes; that his young Queen had borne him a son; and that his horse had won its race at the Olympic Games. But he was not there at Olympias' bedside.

Indeed, he very seldom was. He was too busy. It was still only a few years since the Illyrians had killed King Perdikkas, his elder brother, in battle, with 4,000 other Macedonians, and poured down into the plain to loot, burn and slay. Philip, young, fearless, eloquent, crafty and untiring, had already changed all that; and, to every farmer in the plain of Macedonia, their King's preoccupation with the regions beyond his frontiers must have appeared fully justified. But Olympias did not see it quite like that, especially since Philip consoled himself with a different girl (or girls) on each of his numerous campaigns. Sometimes he even went through a form of marriage. One law for the man and another for the woman was common form in Macedonia, as in Greece (or, as Philip would certainly have put it, in the rest of Greece).

Philip was very charming when he did come home, properly interested in his son, and pleased with Olympias; but he was off again next spring. The kings of the Illyrians in the north-west, Thracians in the east (where Philip had just taken over the Greek mining colony of Krênides, renaming it Philippi) and the Paionians between them, all had been given cause to know severally that Philip was too strong for them; but they hoped that by uniting they might be able to restore the happy and not-so-old days of plunder.

The idea was foredoomed. It was impossible for three independent barbarian chiefs to concert joint operations and start mobilizing the clans in secret; and Philip had not spent four years of his adolescence as a hostage in Thebes, in the days when Thebes had defeated Sparta and was taken seriously by Persia, without learning a good deal about intelligence methods. Philip, with his new model army, its spearmen trained in the Theban manner, was paying a state call on the King of Paionia before even his own tribesmen were ready; and the great coalition was broken up and its leaders reduced to swearing renewed (and separate) oaths of brotherhood with Philip, apparently without serious fighting. For the next year or two Greek historians have little to tell about Philip; but he was not idle, and it would appear that he was reducing great areas in the central Balkans to vassaldom.

So Alexander's first memories were of a house where his mother was very much the mistress, and an affectionate and doting mother to him; while 'father' was a rather remote concept, embodied from time to time in a tired, haggard, but still restless man with one eye (he lost the other in storming an Athenian fortress on the coast, when Alexander was three), who turned up at long intervals, as childhood reckons things, and held noisy and somewhat alarming revels, with a horde of other large, bearded men, who wore their swords even in un-dress, and sometimes drew them upon each other, especially in the torch-lit dining-hall in the late evening, when the drinking had begun at dusk.

Both Philip and his son after him kept up the royal Macedonian feasting and hard-drinking habits; Philip with gusto, Alexander in youth with restraint as far as his own drinking went; later, in Asia, he drank more. If they had not done so, and also led their men personally across battle-fields and up breaches, receiving more wounds in their short lives than almost any man in their armies, they would hardly have kept so effectively the loyalty of their troops. Even so, both of them were threatened again and again by the conspiracies of noblemen; but these were as much part of the life of an Argead King of Macedon as of an early Stuart or a Plantagenet.

Otherwise Philip was far from uncivilized. Macedonian kings were proud of their Greek blood, and it was only jaundiced opponents like Demosthenes the Athenian who ventured to call them 'barbarians'. They claimed descent from Hêrakles through the Dorian Kings of Argos, and they learned the tales of Troy and of Odysseus, and the songs of the Greek lyric poets, as they learned their letters. Fifty years before Alexander was born, a King of Macedon had been proud to give a home to the aged 'modernist' playwright, Euripides, eighty years old and sick and tired of a democracy which had led Athens into defeat and revolution, and whose philistines accused Euripides of preaching atheism and immorality. In Macedonia the old man's genius burst into flame yet once more, and produced *The Bacchanals*, that amazing drama of the northern mystery-religion; full of its sense of power and divine 'possession', giving strength and freedom as of a hind let loose; full of the air of mountain and forest, in which at last the women tear limb from limb the puritan King who had tried to quell their revels.

Olympias herself was a devotee of such mystery-religions; of orgies little less wild than those which Euripides depicted. She, too, had taken part in the Maenad dances under the moon, while great tame serpents raised their heads from the baskets that contained the Sacred Things of the god, or coiled themselves harmlessly round the arms and wands of the women. It was, in fact, at a religious ceremony that she had first met Philip in the island of Samothrace, with its wild mountain scenery, when they were both very young. It was probably when Philip was about twenty, and had time, during his brother's short reign, and after escaping from Thebes, to visit the island and be initiated into the mysteries of the Kabeiroi, those Nibelung dwarfish gods who had something to do with the mysteries of the metal-worker. Olympias, no more than a girl, had come from the home of her father, the King of Epeiros, probably with her brother Arybas, who was King in Philip's time. They were married when Philip was twenty-two, in the year in which Perdikkas fell in battle, and he succeeded to a precarious throne.

It was like Philip, who had always a taste for difficult conquests, to select this fierce witch-woman for his Queen, and no doubt he treated her well according to his lights. She was always left with every possible comfort, and under adequate protection. After all, she was not only very beautiful : she came of one of the oldest and proudest families in the Mainland, tracing their ancestry to Achilles; a family highly desirable as allies, and not likely to put up lightly with casual treatment of their daughters and sisters. But Philip had other things to do than stay dallying with Olympias all the year round; as she, he felt, must surely understand. A king had his place in the world to occupy adequately (that would be the way that Philip looked at it, rather than saying that a king had his duties to perform); and as for his mistresses or temporary wives, how could any reasonable woman possibly expect things to be otherwise?

Where Philip made his mistake was presumably in expecting a woman, especially an Olympias, to be reasonable on just that subject. Philip in general was no mean psychologist; he was no mere brute of an Early Iron Age warrior; he was the greatest diplomat of his day, one whose personal charm, turned on at will, was almost as important in the process of getting his way with Greek envoys and politicians as the liberal distribution of bakshish. As such he was a skilled judge of the feelings of people with whom he had to deal. But the fact remained : Olympias wanted more of Philip than Philip had any intention of giving her. She could never be all – never more than one among many interests – in his life, as she had hoped to be. They drifted gradually apart. They co-operated reasonably well, it would seem, over Alexander's upbringing; but after the girl Cleopatra, born a year after Alexander, she never had another child.

So during the three parts of every year when Philip was away, Olympias brooded over the little Alexander, pampered him and tried to spoil him; whereat Philip, with remarkable dexterity, singled out a suitable male relative of Olympias herself to be the child's tutor and see that she did nothing of the kind. In her dealings with the child, at least, she had every opportunity to try to fulfil her desire to be worshipped, to be everything to somebody. She was successful. Still beautiful, and no more than twenty years older than her son, she seems indeed to have succeeded in saddling him with something of a mother-fixation. It comes out, not unpleasantly, in his dealings with other middle-aged queens, whom he met on his campaigns. Moreover, she, unlike Philip, was no psychologist at all, and it would have been surprising if she had not let drop from time to time in the child's hearing some candid expressions of her views about the child's father and his treatment of herself.

Inevitably in the circumstances, Alexander grew up with what would nowadays be classified as an Œdipus complex. That it was a relatively mild one reflects great credit on Philip. Proud of his son, who already as a small boy was showing marvellous promise, he bent all his great intelligence to the planning of his education; and, most remarkably – for Philip was not accustomed to being crossed by anyone near him, except Olympias – finding Alexander, amid all his brilliance, strong-willed and difficult, he never, at least deliberately, suppressed and overrode him, but always, except in rare moments of impatience, tried to persuade him by an appeal to reason.

Nevertheless, the complex was indubitably there; with a complication, moreover, which had its effect on a whole chapter of world history. Caught young by the violent remarks of his adored mother about his father's unfaithfulness and sexual promiscuity, Alexander appears to have developed a certain disgust with sex in general. It comes out in the puritanical violence with which he rebuked, more than once, officious toadies who tried to sell him harem slaves; and also in a more impor-

tant matter. When, at twenty, he succeeded to the throne, his
father's advisers urged him that he should leave a son behind
him to succeed to the throne of Macedon, before plunging into
the wilds of Asia. But Alexander waved away the suggestion.
It was no time, he said, for a king to be dallying in women's
bowers, when there were such great deeds to do. Years later,
when men flattered him as superhuman, even divine, he used to
say that fatigue and sex were the two things that reminded him
that he was even as other men. He married, probably for political reasons, at twenty-eight; but when, at thirty-three, he died,
he was still childless. His only offspring, the son born after his
death, was made away with after a few years amid the struggles
of ambitious generals; and even if the break-up of so vast an
empire was in any case inevitable, there can be little doubt that
these struggles were worse and more destructive for the fact
that the Macedonian royal family had become extinct.[1]

Alexander's education as a small boy was under the general
direction of Leonidas, 'a man of severe character,' says Plutarch,
'and a kinsman of Olympias.' Leonidas also seems to have been
a man of some breadth of mind, since, for all his royal connections, he did not shun the title of tutor or 'pedagogue'; which,
implying a kind of male nursemaid, was a very humble title in
the Greek social hierarchy. Under him there were masters to
teach reading, writing, arithmetic, geometry, music, riding,
archery, javelin-throwing and all the branches of athletics.
Nearest of all to Alexander's affections, and performing under
Leonidas the nursemaid functions usually assigned to the 'pedagogue', was a certain Lysimachos, from western Greece. He was
no one in particular (says Plutarch again); but he won Alexander's heart by entering into a great 'let's pretend' game, calling
Alexander, Achilles (and indeed, he could soon outrun all his

---

1. The story that he had an older natural son by a Persian mistress
bristles with difficulties and was almost certainly put about by two
of the generals, long after Alexander's death, in support of the
claims of a boy whom they 'ran' (till one of them changed sides and
murdered him instead) as a puppet pretender to the throne; see
p. 185.

playmates), and Philip, Pêleus, and Lysimachos himself, Phoinix, after the 'old knight' whom Pêleus sent to Troy to look after the young Achilles.

It is revealing that the young Alexander always thought of himself as another Achilles, the hero of his mother's family. His father's ancestor Hêrakles had also voyaged to Asia, as well as to all the other corners of the world that Alexander at various times dreamed of; he also had fought his battles – and used intelligence as well as brute force in the achievement of the famous Labours; he also was a hero who had chosen a hard life with honour rather than an easy one, as a famous fable described; but it was not till after he was king that Alexander took up the mythology of his father's family.

As playmates he had the sons not only of Macedonian nobles, but also of various Greek exiles and adventurers – often men of birth and culture – who had grown great in Philip's service. They grew up with him, and they grew up into men of no mean stamp. Among them were Hêphaistion, tall, handsome, athletic, intelligent enough, if of rather conventional mind; Alexander was devoted to him, and he to Alexander; Ptolemy, from the western Macedonian mountains, who founded the dynasty that held Egypt for 300 years; Nearchos, the Cretan, who explored the Indian Ocean; and Harpalos, the young Macedonian feudal prince who, as Lord of the Treasury, was to break faith with Alexander, and be forgiven and restored to office, and to break faith again.

Alexander grew up, like Philip, a person of extraordinary personal magnetism. It seemed to radiate from him. The ancient writers tell of the peculiar 'melting' glance of his eyes, or of the way in which, as Plutarch says, his body seemed to glow. They are evidently trying to describe something which they found it difficult to express. He also grew up, to the delight of Philip, serious-minded, untiring, passionately keen to succeed in any difficult task, and yet more keen the more difficult it was.

He was a great reader, too. He had been early caught by the glamour of the Tale of Troy, like most Greek boys; and he never grew weary of it. As far as the Oxus and the Indus, he carried with him his personal copy of the Iliad, called the Casket Iliad from its richly wrought Persian travelling case. At nights it lay, with his dagger, under his pillow. Moreover, he seriously and in adult life described it as 'a handbook of military conduct'; and as Agamemnon and Nestor had certainly nothing to teach him on tactics, it is clear that what he means is that it taught the lessons of courage and comradeship and the importance of personal leadership in battle. As to other books, a list survives of those which Harpalos sent him, when from far up in Asia he wrote for 'something to read' : one contemporary history – the *Life and Campaigns of Dionysios of Syracuse*, by Philistos, who was also Dionysios' Admiral; a selection of plays (already classic), from the three great tragedians of Athens; and a couple of volumes of modern poetry, the *Dithyrambs* of Telestes and Philoxenos.

Alexander's relations with Aristotle require fuller treatment.

Songs, stories and games were all very well, but Philip had no intention of letting the education of the next King stop there. Practical soldiering and diplomacy could wait, to be learned later at Philip's side. But in the meantime he must have the best secondary education available in the subjects that would be studied by future leaders in Athens or Thebes. He must, in short, be grounded in philosophy and rhetoric; two subjects whose names had a much wider meaning then than they have now after 2,000 years of scholasticism. Philosophy included the entire field of scientific knowledge, and rhetoric meant much more than learning the tricks of journalese. The word 'orator' practically equalled 'politician'; and rhetoric as taught by the greater sophists – free-lance professors – of the time, such as Isokrates, included the application of the lessons of history. Philip appreciated this, probably better than any King of Macedonia before him, as the result of his time at Thebes, in the days when that city, her new democracy led by the dashing Pelopidas and the philosopher-general Epameinôndas, was the leading state in Greece. Pelopidas had come north with an escort – it was hardly an army – to settle the affairs of Macedon, then in confusion, as so often, after the death of

Philip's father and one of the usual invasions of the hill-men. He appears to have succeeded in getting the boy Philip handed over by the Illyrians, who had captured him, purely by moral suasion and the great name of Thebes. He then took him back to Thebes among other Macedonian hostages for his brother's, the new King's, satisfactory behaviour.

But there was also a good deal of idealism in the Thebes of Epameinôndas' day; and Philip received just such a Greek education as he was now to pass on. Philip was no mean orator himself, and there had been times when oratory, he would say, had been as important to him as military skill; especially in the difficult early days, when it was necessary to hold together a depressed and not yet confident army, or to patch up settlements with three enemies at a time in order to be left alone with the fourth.

Philip had heard of a man whose reputation as a teacher, and also for encyclopedic knowledge, seemed all that could be desired. His father Nikomachos, from Stageira on the coast of Philip's enlarged kingdom, had been physician to the Macedonian court. He himself had studied under Plato in his garden-college outside Athens, the Akadêmeia; but the headship of the college on Plato's death had gone to the founder's nephew, Speusippos; so the man of Philip's choice was easily available. He had been spending the last few years with a friend, the Greek ruler of a city in the Troad; but the friend had just been trapped and put to death by the King of Persia. The Stageirite was invited, and came. His name was Aristoteles, better known today as Aristotle.

Philip assigned for the royal school a rural retreat at Mieza, where probably Hêphaistion, Ptolemy, Harpalos and others of the famous 'Companions' were educated too. Four hundred years later, the garden walks where Aristotle and Alexander had strolled, while Aristotle talked and Alexander, no doubt, asked searching questions, were still shown to tourists under the Roman Empire. We know what philosophy (including science) and rhetoric (including history and politics) meant to Aristotle, from Aristotle's own works; but those dry lecture-notes do little justice to the human personality of that famous teacher. Aristotle – it forms no part of the current modern conception of him – was also a poet. Moreover (and it fitted in well with Philip's and Alexander's ideas), he was strongly anti-Persian. There still exists a poem of his, in praise of his friend Hermeias, that ruler of Atarneus in the Troad, who had been captured by the Persians and tortured, and had died without betraying his friends.

Alexander became deeply attached to Aristotle, corresponded with him from Asia, and used to say that he loved him no less than his father, since 'the one had given him life, but the Philosopher had shown him how to live well'.

It must have been during his tutelage by Aristotle that Alexander conceived in detail the great idea, whose realization was to be the work of his short life : the conquest of Persia and the planting of Greek cities at suitable points, to hold the land for Alexander and to acquire a prosperity such as the mountains of Greece could never afford.

It transpired on one occasion, when Philip came back to his capital to find some Ambassadors from Persia awaiting him, that the young Prince had done the honours as host very efficiently, and had also impressed them by the mature and serious way in which he questioned them about their own country; all about the distances from this place to that, and what the roads were like up-country, and whether the Great King was himself a notable warrior, and about the strength and armament of the Persian army. The Persian Ambassadors thought him a charming boy.

Perfectly naturally, Alexander grew up with the idea that conquest on a grand scale was the only life-work for a man such as he meant to be. It is needless to speculate as to his reasons for attacking Persia. As has been well said, 'it never occurred to him not to'. Military operations, moreover, had already been begun, by Philip; and in any case (as we shall see later) the military power built up by Philip was too expensive for the resources of Macedonia, and could only be maintained by continual aggression. Peace, when Alexander came to the throne, meant debt and fierce retrenchment; an alternative to military glory obviously unthinkable to him.

To suppose, in fact, that a ruler like Alexander must have as his reason or excuse for conquest some benefit to mankind or to a nation is to read back into the Greek period the ethics – one need not say of Christianity, but of the Christian era. *The idea that pure self-aggrandizement and desire to dominate is a disreputable motive, which requires cloaking or disguising, has become held in the West as a result of the teaching of Christ.* Plato and other thinkers had seen the vanity of self-aggrandizement; and the give-and-take of life in the Greek cities had led to the spread of ideas of justice and moderation, between citizens of the same Republic. But 'Thou shalt love thy neighbour as thyself' is Jewish (Leviticus). Much less did Greeks – including Aristotle – think of Greeks as having any responsibility towards 'barbarians'.

The ethics which the young Alexander learned from Aristotle – or before – included a high ideal of friendship. Friendship, after all, is natural to man; Alexander could read about it not only in Aristotle but in Homer; and all his soldiers were to some extent his friends. But there is no reason to believe that Alexander at any time had any conception of duty to his neighbour *qua* neighbour or even to his subjects *qua* subjects. Allegiance was owed to him by them; another matter. Even Aristotle in his *Ethics* and *Politics* – lectures intended chiefly for republican citizens – had taught, moreover, that the really great man was more or less a law unto himself, and that the hero-King (is this a later note, with an eye on Alexander?) had no more to do but to become divine ... But in Alexander there was something more primitive too. As with most people, in the last resort his values were those that he had learned at his mother's knee. His one abiding ideal was the glory of Alexander.

At some time in his boyhood happened the famous episode of the horse Boukephalas. Philoneikos of Thessaly, a dealer whom Philip knew quite well, arrived one day with a horse for sale. The price asked was high – thirteen talents, 78,000 day-wages – but Philoneikos not only insisted that this was no ordinary horse, but seemed confident of being able to win the agreement of Philip, who knew as much about horses as he did. Philip went out with Alexander and the officers present to have a personal look at the animal.

The colt was certainly a fine-looking creature; big, for a Greek horse, powerfully built, and black, with a white blaze on the forehead something like the head and horns of an ox; hence his rough-and-ready name, which means 'Oxhead'. But he was nervous too, and his reaction to the presence of a gaily dressed crowd was to become quite unmanageable, so that for some time none of Philip's grooms could get anywhere near him, let alone succeed in mounting. At any suggestion of such liberties, Boukephalas stood straight up on his hind legs, and, as ancient Greek horsemen rode without stirrups, this was a perfectly adequate defence against any approach. Finally, Philip decided that he had no more time to waste, and told Philoneikos to take his animal away. It was at this point that Alexander, who had been standing by muttering such remarks as: 'Fools! Losing a fine horse like that!' broke out into vigorous protest. Philip had so far ignored him. He now turned round upon him and said impatiently: 'Do you really imagine you know more than the grooms, that you think you can manage a horse better than anyone else?'

'I could certainly manage *this* horse better than some people,' retorted Alexander.

'Well,' said Philip, 'then suppose you try and fail, what will you propose as a penalty for pushing yourself forward?'

'I will buy him,' said Alexander.

There was a general roar of laughter among the bystanders, horsemen and horse-copers to a man, and Philip then and there determined to let him try. The odds were all against his breaking his neck, if only because nobody had so far managed even to mount; and if his efforts were an ignominious failure, it might teach his extreme self-confidence a lesson.

'Done,' he said, and father and son proceeded seriously and as men of the world to enter into a formal bet. Alexander went quietly out to the horse, took hold of his bridle-rein and turned his face towards the sun. He had noticed that his shadow (and no doubt also the shadows of the men's fluttering riding cloaks) kept catching his eye, so that he shied and danced whenever anyone went behind his head to mount. Alexander stood for a few moments stroking and patting him. Then he loosed the brooch on his shoulder, and let his riding-cloak fall quietly to the ground. Still stroking him and talking softly, he moved from the horse's head to his neck; patted him on the shoulder, rested his hand there and with a spring was suddenly seated astride him. Still in no hurry, he sat there for a few moments, gently 'feeling his mouth', and then, with a word and a pressure of his heel, set him in motion. Boukephalas went off headlong, with the tremendous acceleration that his owner had promised, leaving Philip standing in anxious silence, while Alexander and the horse disappeared over the plain in a cloud of dust. Alexander, however, had ridden horses almost since he could walk; and Philoneikos, after all, had been prepared to stake his reputation that the beast, though spirited, was not vicious. Once Alexander had gone a few hundred yards, the battle was won. The horse, with the freshness taken out of him, revealed himself as the fine, sensitive animal which had been promised, and which Alexander was to love for many years. It was not many minutes before Alexander, laughing and proud, came back at a more moderate pace, the horse, now apparently a reformed character, answering willingly to the rein. Everyone cheered and applauded, and Philip, with tears in his eyes, kissed Alexander as he dismounted, with the words:

'My son, you must find a Kingdom for yourself; Macedonia is not large enough to hold you.'

Such episodes convinced Philip that he had indeed a son after his own heart; though there were things about Alexander's intellectual interests that were beyond him ... Philip could not resist pulling his leg sometimes; as once after dinner, when Alexander gave such an accomplished performance on the lyre that his soldier father growled, 'Aren't you *ashamed* to play as well as that?'

Philip was immensely proud, as he might well be, of his son.

Alexander for his part respected his father's intellect and prowess. His conscious mind admired Philip; but behind it there was always that half-conscious jealousy which, as Philip's power reached farther and farther, east to the Black Sea, west to the Adriatic, south to the Gulf of Corinth, prompted him to say many a time to Ptolemy and the others : 'Father is going to do everything; at this rate he won't leave any conquests for you and me.'

2 The Men and the Hour
(Greece and Persia, 401–340)

The idea of conquering Persia had been in the air in Greece since before Philip was born.

The old Empire's fate had been sealed, in fact, in 401 B.C., when 14,000 Greek mercenaries in the service of the rebel Prince Cyrus went twice through a Persian army, almost without losing a man; the barbarian infantry – wretched peasant conscripts dragged from the plough to fight in a dynastic quarrel – turning tail in many places before the grim line of spears came anywhere near them. Still more remarkable had been the escape of the bulk of these mercenaries, the famous Ten Thousand, from the heart of Mesopotamia, without cavalry support or archers, without regular commissariat, without maps and without generals, except such as they elected after Cyrus had fallen and their original leaders had been treacherously seized and put to death. It was not only Xenophon the Athenian who was impressed by the achievement, in which he himself had borne a great part. Other writers, like Isokrates, whose pamphlets reached a wide public, and other men of action, like Agêsilaos, King of Sparta, were quick to draw the moral. Agêsilaos, over in Asia to protect the Greek cities of the coast, at the time when the remnants of the Ten Thousand reappeared, took them into his service, and having organized a cavalry force, had dreams of marching into the interior himself; and the King of Persia had no force fit to pit against him.

Persia had other weapons, however – her diplomacy and her gold. Both worked wonders in Greece, where triumphant Sparta, like Athens before her and Thebes after her, had plenty of jealous enemies; and it was thus that, for sixty-seven years, from the march of Xenophon to that of Alexander, Persia kept the Greek enemy at arm's length. In fact she succeeded, as never since the days of Xerxes, in establishing the King as a ruler over the Greeks of Asia, and even, the crowning insult in the eyes of patriots, as arbiter of the quarrels of the Greeks in their homeland. Division, mutual jealousy and the incapacity to combine for an end remoter than tomorrow were the bane of the Greeks in that as in every age.

The Persian Court knew all there was to know about the combination of judicious expenditure with diplomatic politeness. It was assisted further by the fact that many Greeks, who regarded themselves as high-minded public men, saw nothing wrong in accepting presents from foreign governments (and 'present', by the way, is the only word existing in Greek for a bribe), so long as they were not being asked to do anything harmful to the State. A Themistokles, like a Talleyrand, had not the slightest objection to being paid by a foreign power for doing something which he had intended to do anyhow. Nevertheless, this standard of morality was a dangerous one; not only dangerous to the State, but even, on occasions, to the individual envoy, as is shown by the sad story of Timagoras of Athens. Timagoras, falling ill under the rigours of the Persian climate, was told by his doctor that he should have cow's milk. He told the Persians responsible for his entertainment, and next day the King presented him with eighty cows. He was also presented with a luxurious camp bed, complete with a set of slaves to make it for him, lest Greeks might find it too complicated; and when he went home His Majesty had him carried all the way to the coast (about three months' journey) in a litter regardless of expense. But at Athens public opinion thought that Timagoras, overwhelmed by these favours, had not taken a stiff enough line in negotiation. He was brought to trial and actually put to death for corruption, in spite of the efforts of his political supporters, one of whom tried to laugh the matter off by suggesting that the city really ought to select annually, instead of the Board of the Nine Regents (the Archons), nine poor good men and true to serve as Ambassadors to Persia.

Nevertheless, the military weakness of Persia was no secret. Reminders of it were always coming in. A disgruntled Arcadian envoy came back from Persia when Philip was a lad, saying that the King had 'plenty of cooks and bakers and confectioners, and hordes of butlers and porters, but men who could look Greek spearmen in the face he had never seen there, and not for the want of trying'. And even the famous Golden Plane Tree, he added, the treasure of the Imperial Court, was a miserable little thing when you came to see it and hardly big enough for a cricket to take cover on. In fact, theorists like Isokrates probably underestimated the difficulties, both of coping with Persia's powerful cavalry in the great plains of Asia, and of the mere organization of a sizeable army traversing those vast distances. Ambitious generals asked nothing better than to be the leader of an army into Persia; and every idealist pamphleteer – not only Isokrates – dreamed dreams of what might be done if only Greeks could unite against the foreign foe.

Alexander's exploit, like many other deeds that have altered the world, was waiting to be done if only the hour could bring forth the man.

In the parallel case of Columbus – a truly great man, and original enough to be thought a little mad in his time – it is possible to say exactly by whom, and when, America would have been discovered, if he had died young. America would have been discovered by Cabral in the year 1500, on the day when Cabral's squadron, bound for the Indies via the Cape of Good Hope, and cautiously standing well out from the coast of Africa, came entirely unexpectedly within sight of the coast of Brazil. Some other epoch-making achievements have actually been accomplished by two men almost simultaneously: Newton and Leibnitz wrangled over their priority in discovering the calculus; Darwin had almost finished *The Origin of Species* when A. R. Wallace sent him his own essay on the subject; Adams and Leverrier independently discovered the planet Neptune; and in our time independent intervention has become common enough to keep a whole corps of patent lawyers in considerable opulence. The best part of Napoleon's work, it is generally agreed, would have been carried out had he fallen at Lodi, probably by Hoche or Moreau.

In the case of the Hellenization of the East, it is not possible to say precisely who would have done the work if Alexander, like Philip, had been killed too soon; but it is possible to say that not only had many a man dreamed of the great project *in vacuo*, but that several men of action had come within measurable distance of attempting it, before the changes and chances of politics cut short their careers. Agêsilaos of Sparta had 'made the Great King tremble in his shoes', according to a speaker in Xenophon, before Persia managed to stir up trouble for him in Greece; but the man who came nearest to anticipating Alexander was the Thessalian, Jason of Pherai.

Jason's career ended with his assassination a little before the time when Philip went as hostage to Thebes. Before that, starting as Lord of Pherai (inland from modern Volo) he had made himself overlord of Thessaly and of the surrounding mountain tribes as far as Thermopylæ. The King of Epeiros was his ally, and had apparently acknowledged Jason as in some fashion his suzerain; and with Thessaly for once firmly united, and Macedonia, as often, weak and divided, Jason's influence was strong in Macedonia too. His army, as overlord of Thessaly (a position recognized by Thessalian law, though perhaps, like the Roman dictatorship, only in emergencies), was computed by him at 8,000 cavalry, and 20,000 pikemen, of which 6,000 horse and 10,000 foot represent the regular levy of Thessaly, and the rest may have been his own mercenaries. For light-armed men he could raise unlimited mountaineers, whose ancestral weapons were target and javelin, from Olympos, Ossa, Pêlion and Pindos.

For his own part, Jason was one of the greatest soldiers of his age. An opponent, in Xenophon's *History*, pays tribute to his mastery of the three great methods of generalship – deception, speed and violence of attack – and continues: 'He can work day and night, and when he is in a hurry he goes on working straight through his meals; he thinks that the right time to rest is when he has got where he wants to be and has done what needs doing; and he has accustomed all his men to the same standards. Moreover, he has the completest self-control of any man I know, so that he is not likely to fail through personal weaknesses.'

To serve under such a captain was an object of competition to ambitious professional soldiers. It was no easy service. Jason's rule was : 'No one is allowed in this army who cannot do what I do,' and if you could not stand Jason's pace, you could go elsewhere. But the rewards were great : *esprit de corps*, pride in one's service, extra pay for merit, even sickness and burial insurance. Jason rarely let his mercenaries loose on a population to enjoy themselves; he preferred to pay well. He was a man of limitless ambition, matching his tremendous powers; the project of uniting Greece and conquering Persia is explicitly ascribed to him, and as Xenophon died before the rise of Philip, what he says about Jason is *not* a mere matter of reflecting back into the past what was done later. At the same time, Jason was no monster like the conventional tyrant of Greek fables; no horror-stories are told of him, and he appears to have won the admiration and confidence of the democratic hero of Thebes, Pelopidas, the same who took Philip as a hostage.

Jason, in short, sounds more than a little like Alexander, and the forces that he could raise were actually greater than the recorded numbers of cavalry and armoured infantry in Alexander's expeditionary force.

Persia meanwhile had probably weakened since the days of Dareios and Xerxes. Her cavalry were still formidable, but one hears nothing now of the former Median and Persian foot-archers, accustomed to pour their arrows from behind the fence of their wicker shields, and if necessary, though less heavily armed than Greeks, to fight it out at close quarters with their short swords, holding the enemy till, according to the standard plan, the overwhelming Persian cavalry could come in on a flank. The infantry of the last Dareios were of a different stamp; the best of them, wild mountaineers, or imitation Greek men-at-arms, or, so far as money could buy them, actual Greek mercenaries, brave and formidable, but with obvious disadvantages.

One wonders why. The decline is probably connected with the enormous hoards of gold and silver which Alexander was to capture at Susa and Persepolis. The Great King's bullion reserve amounted to 180,000 talents, equivalent, even if the amount is reckoned in Greek *silver* talents, to 1,080,000,000 Athenian silver drachmas; over 200 times that of Athens at the start of the Peloponnesian War. In fact, its reckless dispersal by Alexander, in rewards to henchmen and pay for troops, caused a kind of inflation, with formidable social repercussions in the Greek world. In other words, Persian taxation had been steadily taking gold out of circulation throughout the Empire. Such a process, *while taxes presumably remained at traditional levels* for generations at a time, could not have failed gradually to squeeze out the middle class, the small farmers of Iran, transforming them into serfs or hirelings of the richer, more powerful and economically better able to survive. A similar process happened under the Roman Empire; and in Persia we know at least that many of the noble families, whose heads had often become *de facto* hereditary princes of the provinces originally allotted to them in trust, were now not only officials or Lords Marchers, but also landed proprietors on an enormous scale. The troops produced by such a social system naturally were such as Alexander found before him : cavalry, brave and formidable, but not unlimited in numbers; infantry, poor; leadership, brave and chivalrous, but marked, at least at first, by a headlong and courageous stupidity that seems to be the prerogative of a feudal nobility.

It is worth remarking that the only formidable contingent of Iranian tribal infantry, armed in the old fashion, that fought against Alexander, was that of the Mardian Archers; mountaineers who, from poverty and by armed resistance, had succeeded in remaining free peasants, paying little if any tribute to the Great King.

Meanwhile, Greece also was going through a social and economic crisis which left it ripe, if it could not unite, for a great imperialist enterprise; or doomed, alternatively, to formidable internal struggles. Population, to judge by the strength of citizen armies, was already beginning, in some of the more 'progressive' cities, to decline. In Sparta, with her unique 'national socialism', the governing class was decreasing rapidly; we have no figures for the Helots. Wild and backward Arcadia, on the other hand, had astonished the generation before Philip by her teeming manpower and the marching and fighting powers of her young men; and it was from Arcadia and from the still wilder valleys of the northern Pindos that there came most of the supply of tough Greek mercenaries, ready to fight under a Jason, under the King of Persia, or alongside the citizen troops of Athens, Thebes, Sparta or any state that would pay them.

Who were these mercenaries socially? Chiefly, it appears, younger sons, or in any case landless men whom their home valleys could no longer support; while the wars of recent generations, though relatively innocuous as regards cities and villages actually destroyed, certainly helped to increase the numbers of those uprooted men, whom Isokrates describes as 'now wandering through indigence . . . and a danger to any population that comes in their way'. Greece had got, in fact, a dangerous, growing, armed and warlike proletariat; and Isokrates, in his old age, taking up again, in a pamphlet addressed to Philip, the idea which in youth he had hoped to see realized by Athens and Sparta, begs him urgently to undertake the great enterprise soon; to seize either the whole Persian Empire, or at least Asia Minor 'from Cilicia to Sinôpe', and to found cities in which to settle those now wandering – a menace to the prosperous bourgeois society that Isokrates knew.

While the social system of Greece reached this crisis, the Greek Age of Reason had had its effect on the art of war, as on every walk of life. The traditional method of fighting, which had hitherto evolved slowly through the centuries under the unconscious guidance of social developments, improvements in metallurgy and the geography of Greece, was now transformed swiftly by a generation of professional captains, who thought things out. Armament was especially improved by the Athenian Iphikrates, reorganizer of the 'peltast', a type of light infantryman, faster and more active than the traditional heavy 'hoplite' with his armour and six-foot spear; now re-equipped with a light shield and light but efficient mountain boots, evolved after much thought by Iphikrates himself; with a nine-foot spear, against the old six-foot weapon, and a sword with a blade of thirty inches or more, as compared with the traditional leaf-shaped sword only half that length. The latter was actually a Bronze Age shape, suitable to a metal too brittle to make a long cutting (as opposed to thrusting) blade, and maintained in vogue by pure conservatism up to the Age of Reason.

At the same time, tactics had been developed, especially the use of light-armed infantry with bows or javelins against heavy infantry; the use of shock action by cavalry; above all, the use of different arms in combination. And, most important of all, Epameinôndas, the intellectual general whom the young Philip had known at Thebes, had been the first to formulate consciously the principle of superiority of force *at the decisive point*, not necessarily over the whole field of operations. Applying that principle on the decisive field of Leuktra, where he was outnumbered by the dreaded Spartans and their allies, he attacked the Spartans themselves (holding the right wing of their army, as they had done for centuries) with his own highly trained Thebans, transferred – a revolutionary move – to his left. Meanwhile he kept his centre and right, formed of faint-hearted allies, écheloned back, calculating rightly that if the Thebans could defeat the Spartans, there would be no need to bring his less trustworthy troops into action at all.

Epameinôndas', too, was the 'indirect approach', which we shall see Alexander employ on several fields : the oblique advance, threatening to fall upon the enemy's flank, and then, if, as was to be expected, the enemy tried to conform, the sudden swoop upon him while caught in the act of an unpremeditated and therefore less orderly move.

Philip, throughout his career, applied the principle of economy of force, overwhelming strength at the decisive point and none wasted anywhere – and those of speed, deception and surprise, for which Jason of Pherai had been famous. At the same time he made continual efforts and experiments in the improvement of arms and tactics. The result, by the time he died, was the production of the finest hoplite infantry ever seen. The long spear introduced by Iphikrates had been increased, perhaps to eleven feet; and drill, essential if a phalanx using the long pike were to have any flexibility, had been perfected to a degree beyond anything seen before, even at Sparta.

Philip's skill in the exploitation of every slight advantage appears already, in that first decisive battle against the Illyrians, which opened the Macedonian army's career of conquest, and which, curiously, is almost the only one of Philip's battles of which we have a clear tactical picture. There were about 10,000 infantry on each side, and the Macedonians were simply the old territorial levy, not the professional army of ten years later. In quality they were probably in no way superior to the Illyrians. But Philip had 600 horse against 500, and the Macedonian cavalry, armoured nobles on well-nourished horses from rich meadows of the Vardar, probably were more formidable man for man. The advantage was enough for Philip. He drove away the Illyrian cavalry, kept his own men in hand, wheeled them and brought them in, in one mass, on the flank of the enemy's infantry, already engaged in front. Over 7,000 Illyrians fell in the battle and the pursuit. It was an ample revenge for the bloody defeat of Perdikkas two years before, and the event which above all made Philip at twenty-three the hero of the Macedonian people.

Alike in Philip's 'crowning mercy' at Chaironeia, and in all Alexander's pitched battles, we shall see, *mutatis mutandis*, the same fundamental plan – the application of Epameinôndas' principles by an army strong in cavalry.

3 The Prince
(340–336)

By the time he was sixteen, Alexander, if he had by no means learned all that Aristotle knew, had acquired at any rate, a quite unusual knowledge of the history of Greece, its current affairs and the geography, climate, products, flora, fauna and armies of most neighbouring countries. He knew also something of mathematics, astronomy and natural history. He had a genuine disinterested curiosity about these matters, as well as an appreciation of their usefulness. In Asia he took with him scientific experts who collected data and specimens, which were placed at Aristotle's disposal. An odd detail shows Aristotle's influence perhaps even more strikingly: he took a particular interest in medicine, and was very fond of prescribing for and dosing his friends. It may have been partly a trick caught from his mother; but biology was, of all fields, that in which Aristotle was pre-eminent.

But at sixteen there came an end to school and free reading and holidays and argumentative walks with Aristotle in the gardens at Mieza. Philip judged his son grownup; and when he set off for the campaign that was to complete his control of Balkan Europe up to the Sea of Marmara, he left Alexander as his deputy in charge of Macedonia. It is sometimes assumed that Alexander at sixteen would only be a titular viceroy; but Alexander's character, and Philip's knowledge of Alexander's character, hardly make that likely. No doubt he had as his Chief of Staff one of Philip's best generals – probably Antipatros, whom Alexander himself left in charge of Macedonia later – but Alexander at sixteen was not likely to be a puppet.

There is no reason to think that he 'left school' with any

regret. On the contrary, from the whole bent of his character, he must have welcomed the opportunity for coping with real situations and giving real executive orders. He probably hoped that something would happen in his father's absence that would give him a real crisis to deal with; and something did. For Philip, not for the first or second time in his life of difficult achievements, failed in his enterprise of this year.

Philip was attacking Perinthos, on the Sea of Marmara. His battering rams, covered by great penthouses moving on wheels, shook the walls, covered by the fire of a powerful light artillery of catapults and magnified crossbows; his sappers undermined them. Whole sections of wall came crumbling down, and the Macedonians stormed the breaches. Presently the whole wall was in Philip's possession; but not the town. Philip was faced by the resistance of free men defending their hearths and homes. Perinthos, like most Greek cities was built on a site selected for defence. Its houses rose tier above tier, up the inward slope of a rocky peninsula, and the front grew narrower and narrower as one advanced. The narrow lanes that led up between the houses were barricaded at every turn; the approach up every barricaded alley was overlooked by snipers from roofs and windows, with javelins, arrows or plain brickbats; and if the walls of the houses were less solid than that of the town, it was practically impossible to bring up the great rams over ground encumbered with ruins. The Macedonians attacked in relays, by day and night, trying to tire the defenders out by the sheer continuity of their assault. But reinforcements were by this time reaching Perinthos from Byzantium, which felt itself equally menaced, and even mercenaries and supplies from the Persian governors across the Straits. It became clear at last that Perinthos could not be taken, or not for any price that Philip was ready to pay; he drew off the quickest-moving troops in his army and marched rapidly on Byzantium, hoping to find it half-garrisoned and unprepared.

He failed again, baulked of a night surprise by a strange light in the sky, which was at once ascribed to divine intervention and may, it is suggested, have been the Aurora Borealis. Athens, too, stirred up at last to action by the fierce harangues of Demosthenes, was beginning to intervene. Chares, her favourite *condottiere*, appeared with a squadron of ships which drove off Philip's light galleys. He was followed by Phôkion, her best citizen-general, with a full hundred sail. Philip 'pulled out'; it was only 'like the ram, to butt harder' (a saying of Philip's own); but his prestige had suffered a check, and repercussions in his great northern hinterland, of which the Greeks knew little, were such as to cause him to spend the next twelve months campaigning in the interior.

It was in this crisis that Alexander fought his first independent campaign, when during his Lieutenancy of the Realm, a northern tribe, the Maidoi, revolted. Alexander marched against them, experiencing for the first time the delight of the command of an army, of which he had dreamed since boyhood; defeated them, and following Philip's custom, planted a city – a walled military outpost – among them, which he called Alexandropolis. Some royal fathers might have objected that this was too previous.

His next recorded campaign was a sterner test.

Tireless as ever, Philip returned from the north victorious over the Triballoi, the toughest of the Balkan tribes, but temporarily crippled by a wound. It must have been from his sickbed that he directed the diplomatic operations by which, almost before Athens had contradicted the usual reports that he was dead, Philip himself was down in central Greece intervening once more on behalf of the God of Delphi – an admirable propaganda line – against the 'impious' Lokrians of Amphissa, who had dared to cultivate land belonging to Apollo. Restored to health, about the autumn of 339, Philip swept down through Thessaly, where, says Isokrates, he had brought it to pass that the people trusted him better than any of their own leaders; through Thermopylæ, unguarded against him since, seven years earlier, he had overthrown the Phokians to the south of it – also on the charge that they had laid impious hands on the treasures of Apollo – and through Phokis, where there was now no one to say him nay. But, arrived in Phokis, he took, not the road towards Delphi, but the road to Thebes and Athens.

All the time both Philip and his agents abroad were playing his usual 'political warfare' game – promising to Thebes, his old ally against Phokis, that all he asked was passage through her territory to chastise his old enemy, Athens; and to Athens (not without sincerity, strange to say), that he would not dream of harming such a revered and almost sacred city. For once, however, he was defeated in diplomacy. Thebes, at last, was thoroughly alarmed, and Demosthenes won the greatest success of his life when he persuaded her to throw in her lot with Athens against Philip, now repairing fortifications and making himself a forward base at Elateia in Phokis.

So it came to pass that, after a winter 'war of positions' in the valley – really a narrow plain – of the Boiotian Kephisos, by the western gate of Boiotia at Chaironeia, Alexander found himself sitting his horse at the head of his father's cavalry, on the left of the line, looking across the plain at the two-mile front of the allied armies of Thebes, Athens, Megara, Corinth and Achaia. The forest of spears and long line of round shields was flanked by cavalry and peltasts. And all information, as well as all probability, indicated that the citizen troops of Thebes, who took their training seriously, and had long been accounted the most formidable infantry of their day, were on the enemy's right, facing Alexander.

Of the decisive battle we know disappointingly little. Pictures have been drawn of the Thebans and Athenians with their six-foot spears struggling vainly to get anywhere near the Macedonians, armed with the sarissa; but Thebans and Athenians of that age were so lacking in military sense as to have failed altogether to follow the evolution of Philip's armaments.

Where Philip did have an advantage was in drill; and even so, it was a severe struggle. While Philip even gave ground before the fierce initial onslaught always to be expected of the Athenians, letting their young troops wear themselves out against the deadly, yielding front of his veterans, he had given to Alexander the post of honour and glory, the leadership of his attacking wing. And there Alexander won his first great battle. He must have driven the Theban cavalry away first, by superior weight, numbers and hard fighting; and then, with Philip's disciplined cavalry still well in hand, have checked them, wheeled them and brought them in on the flank of the devoted Theban infantry, already held by the Macedonian infantry in their front. Their general, Theagenes, was killed; the Sacred Band of Thebes fell in their ranks, as Philip saw them afterwards, dead, in formation. The Greek right was shattered, and the rest of their line then helplessly 'rolled up'. The Achaians in the centre were almost cut to pieces; and lastly the advancing Athenians were taken in flank and rear. Over 1,000 of their 7,000 or 8,000 men were killed, 2,000 taken prisoner. Demosthenes himself, his political enemies were unfairly quick to point out, was one of those who ran fast enough to get away.

There was no pursuit, Philip's political warfare agents made much of this, as a proof of his magnanimity towards his fellow-Hellenes. In fact, there were good material reasons for it, since Philip's victorious left wing had had first of all to overcome the Thebans, and then fought its way – literally, fighting all the way – for a couple of miles, destroying successive divisions of the Allied infantry, to end the day facing to its original right flank or rear. Most of Philip's army must have ended the day forming a horse-shoe round the last mass of Athenian and allied spearmen. The Allied losses in killed had also been very heavy. There was little to be gained by pursuing the routed men – scarcely a formed unit among them – who were escaping on the road to Thebes.

A characteristic story of Philip is told, concerning the night after the battle: of how he got roaring drunk, as no doubt he had done many a time before, after victories almost as bloody; how he reeled out with a merry party of his generals and 'Companions' to have a look at the corpses, singing raucously the words:

'Demosthenes, Demosthenous, Paianian,[1] proposed ...' which

1. 'Demosthenes, son of Demosthenes, of the parish of Paiania'; the orator's 'full name and address' as given in official documents.

were the first words of the Athenian decree declaring war on Philip, and happened to make a rather good jingling iambic line; and of how – and this also is characteristic – an Athenian politician well known to him, Dêmades, who had always belonged to the pro-Macedonian peace party, but had played his part in the Athenian ranks when it came to war, and been captured, sobered him with the words:

'The Gods have given you the part of Agamemnon to play, King Philip, but you seem to prefer that of Thersîtes.'

Alexander does not appear in this episode, and one wonders where he was. He was only eighteen; he had charged with the cavalry at least twice, had been in two serious *mêlées*, had perhaps killed for the first time, and then had taken part in the final rush to cut off the Athenians. He was probably asleep.

Philip was far too good a politician to have any ideas of holding down the whole of an unwilling Greece by Macedonian garrisons at all strategic points. It is a remark which he might easily have made himself, that you can do anything with bayonets, except sit on them. Philip had no desire for such a throne. Nor would the manpower of Macedonia have been sufficient. On the contrary, Philip tried all his life to placate all Greeks who could be placated, and he sought for himself nothing more nor less than the Captaincy of such a League, to carry Greek arms into Persia, as Isokrates and many others had so long proposed. On the morrow of the battle, his political emissaries were already busy making overtures for the formation of a League of United Greek States.

At the same time, with an eye to the short as well as to the long run, he was at pains to divide Athens from Thebes, by imposing such peace terms as should placate the former – a city which Philip had always respected and in which there was a strong peace party – while firmly holding down the latter, a state which was both unpopular among its neighbours and physically easier for a Macedonian garrison to hold. Thebes had to see a Macedonian garrison installed on her citadel, which implied control of her government. The two cities at opposite ends of Boiotia, Plataia and Orchomenos, which Thebes had destroyed, were to be restored. Their inhabitants could be trusted to pursue a good anti-Theban policy, and, the most cunning stroke of all, Thebes was made to cede to Athens the border territory of Orôpos, the bone of contention in endless border wars. As 'compensation' for this bounty, Philip required Athens to surrender the Gallipoli peninsula, which he required as a jumping-off ground for the next act on his programme ...

For the rest, Philip showed towards Athens an astonishing generosity – and saw to it that it was well publicized. He restored his Athenian prisoners without ransom (not, we must suppose, immediately, but as part of a peace treaty by which Athens entered into formal alliance with him); and he sent back the ashes of their dead, after honourable cremation on the battlefield, accompanied by a military guard of honour under Antipatros and Alexander.

This was probably the only time in his life that Alexander visited Athens.

Philip himself marched on with his army through western Attica to Corinth and the Peloponnese. Most of the secondary cities of central Greece had felt the weight of his hand at Chaironeia. The others, those which had taken the Macedonian side from the start, were congratulating themselves on their foresight and on their correct judgement of Philip as a good and generous Hellene. With every state Philip made a separate treaty; there was no general treaty between Philip and the Greeks, which might have assisted the discontented in any efforts to form a common front against him. Only Sparta, proud as ever, though now impotent in her corner of the Peloponnese, still stood out and refused to negotiate. Philip marched down through Arcadia and into the plain of the Eurôtas, his army reinforced by allied contingents of Argives, Messenians, Arcadians – all Sparta's old enemies. Sparta's territory was ravaged and disputed border lands taken from her and given to her neighbours. It is not clear whether in the end Philip took the trouble to make peace with her at all. Certainly he never considered outraging Greek feeling by destroying, as he could have destroyed, that unbeautiful, unwalled, untidy city, which, almost as much as Athens, had become a pan-Hellenic institution. Moreover, it would have been unlike Philip not to calculate that Argos, for example, was much more likely to remain a good ally so long as she had not only had the debatable land of Kynouria to cultivate, but a vindictive and unforgiving Sparta against whom to hold it.

The separate treaties with each state were the basis of Philip's predominance. Meanwhile, Greek feeling, ever sensitive, as Philip well knew, was to be placated by the spectacle of free and equal membership for all, in a League which was to put an end to the eternal and fratricidal border wars, and which had a positive common object – a thing the lack of which has contributed to the unsuccess of many another League in history – in the prosecution of the national, imperialistic and frankly predatory war against Persia. Revenge for the outrages committed by Xerxes, was the cry. Privately, poor men thought of well-paid service as mercenaries, of good farms as colonists, of good openings in business or posts under the government; and many rich men thought, if we may judge by Isokrates, what a good thing if all these formidable mercenaries and hungry proletarians could be drawn off elsewhere.

The negotiations at Corinth were protracted. Philip must have worked hard, giving endless audiences and using his famous charm upon potentially useful or troublesome politicians and *condottieri*. But the next summer saw him back in Macedonia, preparing already for the great expedition. And here another thing befell which shows once more the hot-blooded man in Philip that sometimes interfered with the best-laid schemes of Philip the King. Philip fell in love, not for the first, second or twentieth time; contracting, apparently, a *grande passion* for Cleopatra, niece of his general, Attalos, one of the corps commanders designated for Asia.

The niece of Attalos, a great Macedonian noble, could not simply become one of Philip's temporary concubines. It was to be honourable marriage or nothing; but honourable marriage meant something which Olympias clearly must have designated in quite other terms. Philip, however, had long ceased taking any notice of Olympias' tantrums. He let her remain in her apartments. Everything was arranged, and a great wedding feast took place in Philip's hall. Everyone drank deep, according to Macedonian custom, and at a fairly advanced stage in the proceedings Attalos, a proud man, rose, apparently to propose the health of the bride and bridegroom. In the course of his speech he called upon the Macedonians to pray to the gods that of Philip and Cleopatra there might be born a legitimate son as successor to the kingdom.

Thus far Alexander, sitting among his friends on the other side of the hall, had grimly held his peace. This was the point where he boiled over. He rose, shouting: 'What of me, villain? Do you take me for a bastard?' And with that he threw his wine cup in Attalos' face. Philip sprang up, sword in hand, and made for Alexander, but being considerably drunk and the room being encumbered with the small Greek tables that stood at the head of each dining-couch (courses were changed at a Greek dinner by removing these tables with everything on them), he caught his foot in something and fell flat on the floor.

'Look, men!' shouted Alexander. 'Here is the man who is preparing to cross from Europe into Asia, and he can't get from one couch to another without falling down.'

That, rather surprisingly, was as far as the matter went. Presumably Alexander was hustled out of the dining-hall by his friends, and by the light of morning Philip may have felt that his son had some excuse. But for Alexander there was no staying in Macedon. He took Olympias and a few of his friends – they probably included Ptolemy, Harpalos and the three Greeks, Nearchos, Erigyios of Mytilene and his brother Laomedon – and went off over the mountains a few days' journey to her old home in Epeiros.

There he settled his mother with her relations, while he himself went north and lived for a time among the old enemies of his house, in Illyria. The Illyrians had no personal blood-feuds against him; and a discontented Prince of Macedonia was no doubt welcome, being potentially useful either as a hostage or as a pretender to the Macedonian throne.

However, Alexander's exile did not last long. Dêmarâtos of Corinth, one of Philip's Greek officers, prevailed upon the King to make overtures to Alexander, went personally to Illyria, and brought him home. Alexander may well have had more trouble in escaping from the Illyrians than in obtaining a welcome among them; but of this history tells nothing.

Within a very short time he quarrelled with his father again. On this occasion, however, it was not such a serious matter, and was soon made up. The subject this time concerned the marriage of Alexander himself.

Pixodar, Prince of Karia in south-west Asia Minor, was one of the numerous vassals of the King of Persia, with whom Philip was in correspondence. There had just been an anti-Persian democratic revolution in the neighbouring Ephesos, and the victorious democrats appealed to Philip for protection. Philip took the matter seriously and sent a force under his best marshal, Parmenion; and the grateful citizens set up his statue in their great temple of Artemis – 'Diana of the Ephesians'. Pixodar had estimated correctly the balance of military power; and the better to ingratiate himself with Philip, he now offered the hand of his eldest daughter in marriage to one of Philip's sons. Philip agreed; but he had no intention of marrying a minor Asiatic princess to his heir. The son he selected was a certain Arrhidaios, who was base-born and also unbalanced (perhaps epileptic). Alexander, however, still suspicious and upset, goaded by unwise friends and by his mother, who kept sending him letters very hostile to Philip, got the idea that this was again a plan to settle the kingdom upon someone else. He got into touch with Pixodar on his own account, pointing out Arrhidaios' disadvantages as a son-in-law, and suggesting that Pixodar should marry his daughter to Alexander himself.

Pixodar was delighted; but Philip inevitably soon got to know of the intrigue – a pretty kettle of fish. But he kept his temper, which must have cost him a considerable effort, and is one more example of his patience with Alexander. He went to Alexander's room privately, with one witness only, one of Alexander's companions, Philôtas, son of Parmenion, and spoke to him bitterly and severely, but as man to man, asking him what he thought he was doing, and whether he really thought so little of himself as to propose himself for the son-in-law of a prince of the despised race of Karia, who was not even a free man, but a slave of the Great King. Alexander bowed his head, though it must have been a bitter pill for him to swallow; but Philip had had enough of his Greek and Macedonian friends' meddling in state affairs which were also family matters, and sent the whole set, Harpalos, Nearchos, Erigyios and Ptolemy, into exile *sine die*.

Preparations for the great expedition were meanwhile in full swing. Parmenion had met with a reverse inland of Ephesos, at the hands of Memnon of Rhodes, the Persian King's best Greek general; but another force under Parmenion and Attalos now crossed the Dardanelles to secure a bridgehead. This included the whole Asiatic side of the Straits as far as the great port of Kyzikos, in its strong position on the neck of the peninsula. Philip was not the man to proceed without making sure of his foundations in Europe, however. It was necessary to reach an understanding with his western neighbour, King Alexander of Epeiros, the brother of Olympias; all the more so since this Alexander was himself a great warrior, with ambitions for conquest little smaller than Philip's own. He showed no signs of making trouble, however; any diplomatic representations he may have thought it necessary to make on behalf of his sister were given a friendly answer, and the alliance between the kingdoms, it was arranged, was to be cemented by the marriage of the King of Epeiros to his niece, another Cleopatra, the only other child of Philip and Olympias. Under whatever 'gentlemen's agreement' accompanied this marriage, Alexander of Epeiros turned his arms westward to Italy, to win fame and victories against Lucanians and Samnites before he fell a victim to the fickleness and divisions of the Greeks of south Italy, and to the sword of a deserter.

Just enough is known of Alexander's sister to make it plain that in Epeiros, in the ensuing crises, she showed all the force of character and administrative ability that might have been expected of her family, and was fully a match for her formidable mother.

But that is another story. Meanwhile, before Philip should march away, the wedding feast of his daughter was arranged, with festivities on the most magnificent scale at the old capital at Aigai. Guests were invited from every part of Greece; official guests from the Greek Republics and from the kingdoms of the mainland, and private friends of many of the Macedonian nobility. It was to be Philip's great final demonstration of magnificence and hospitality, to impress the Greek world before he set off on the great adventure.

Of course, Philip also consulted the Delphic Oracle; that was in keeping with the policy, which he had pursued for so many years, of appearing as Defender of the Faith, as it were; the great Champion of Apollo, the God's devoutest worshipper. The Oracle's response was all that could be expected:

'Crowned to the altar comes the Bull;
the sacrificer stands.'

Philip was fully satisfied with it. The obvious meaning was that the King of Persia was about to fall like a poleaxed ox before Philip's army. Afterwards, the Greeks noted with suitable sentiments the fact that, like most responses from Delphi, this response was capable of other meanings besides the obvious one.

Long before dawn the people filled the theatre for the sacred dramatic and musical contests, which for Philip, as for his son after him, were an essential part of all festivities.

At daybreak the celebration began. The King and his train approached in solemn procession, headed by the images of the Twelve Gods, gorgeously arrayed. After them came Philip, dressed simply in white, and walking all alone, having bidden his guards to follow him at a distance; he wished to show himself before the eyes of all Greece, not guarded like a tyrant, but protected by the love of his people. The images of the gods turned the corner leading into the theatre, Philip (as though thirteenth among the gods, people whispered) following alone.

And then a young man ran out from the side – he was himself a guardsman, or had been, and no one had challenged him – and, almost before Philip could turn, had stabbed him with a broad Keltic knife that he produced from inside his clothing and ran for the gate. The guards dashed after him, headed by Attalos (back from Asia for the occasion), with Perdikkas and Leonnâtos, names to be famous in Alexander's wars; but there were two horses picketed outside the gate, and the young man, who had evidently known all about the arrangements for the procession, seemed likely to reach them and get clear away. And then his bootlace caught in a bush; he stumbled and fell, and Perdikkas' spear transfixed him before he could rise.

But there was no helping Philip. He was quite dead.

4 King Alexander

(Greece and the Balkans, 336–5)

A Macedonian king's position rested upon acceptance by the people, as expressed by acclamation by the Macedonian army. The first thing to be done was to gain that acclamation.

Almost before the bodies of Philip and his assassin had been carried from the theatre, Alexander was on the stage, handsome, ready-tongued and dominant; not claiming the monarchy, but assuming that it was his. He called upon his people to be calm and undismayed. All things would be administered exactly as under his father. 'Nothing,' he ended, 'has changed, except the name of the King.'

Soldiers and people cheered, and officers and chieftains crowded round Alexander to show their support. Among those whom Alexander must have seen with particular relief was his namesake, Alexander son of Aëropos, heir of the once formidable kings of Lynkestis, in the Florina highlands. Philip had made an end of this and all other such more-or-less-vassal highland kingdoms; and Lynkestis, Orestis, Elymiotis and the rest became provinces. Chieftains who submitted with a good grace were rewarded with positions of power in the new Greater Macedonia, like Perdikkas of Orestis, and Harpalos of Elymiotis; but the House of Lynkestis was proudest of them all, and some of its supporters still aspired to see it rule Macedonia.

Surrounded by his officers, Alexander passed through the still thunderstruck crowd and returned to the palace. There was much to do.

The assassin was dead, and that ended the chance of getting anything out of him as to the background of the crime. He was a young man named Pausanias, who after a quarrel with a protégé of Attalos had been grossly maltreated by that officer and a mob of his horse-boys. Philip, not to offend his generals, had declined to take any interest in his young guardsman's complaint ... But all this had occurred years before; and, moreover, Pausanias had had accomplices. Someone, unremarked, had placed those horses ready behind the theatre. And the murderer had been well informed as to Philip's plan for the procession. Philip had trusted too far. But it did look as if Pausanias had been only a cat's-paw for some persons unknown.

Who they might be left plenty of room for speculation. Agents of Persia? If so, they had covered their approaches well. Or disgruntled ex-chieftains, perhaps of the house of Aëropos? Or Olympias' party, afraid of the growing influence of Attalos? Malicious gossip did not fail to suggest the guilt of Alexander himself.

However it might be, Alexander's first preoccupation was to secure his throne. He struck out, not indiscriminately, but ruthlessly. The two brothers of Alexander son of Aëropos were arrested and put to death, apparently on the vaguest suspicion; but on general principles they were counted too dangerous to live. Their brother was spared, and kept his position in the army, thanks to his prompt support of Alexander, and also to the fact that he was son-in-law to the veteran marshal Antipatros. Two other victims, sacrificed purely for dynastic reasons, were Karânos, a natural son of Philip, and Amyntas, son of Philip's elder brother, the late King Perdikkas, whom Philip had supplanted, and who might therefore reasonably claim to be the rightful king.

There was at no time anything quixotic about Alexander where his personal position was concerned.

Foreign affairs next needed immediate attention. Thrace, Illyria, the Greek states, in fact the entire Balkan peninsula, were in a fever of excitement, and everywhere men were dreaming of throwing off the still new Macedonian yoke. At Athens, where the Assembly had very recently decreed that any conspirator against Philip, if found on Athenian territory, should be extradited, Demosthenes appeared garlanded and in white festal robes, referring to Alexander as 'Margites' – the hero of a famous mock-heroic parody; and a decree was passed awarding posthumous honours to Pausanias. The Thebans were preparing to free their citadel; Ambrakia, on the west coast road, drove out her garrison; the warlike Aitolians recalled the politicians exiled at Philip's demand. Over in Asia, a counter-revolution at Ephesos let in Memnon's army.

Moreover, Demosthenes made secret overtures to Attalos, now back with his troops in Asia, whose quarrel with Alexander at the wedding of Philip and Cleopatra was public property, and who might well cherish ambitions for a regency on behalf of his infant great-nephew, Cleopatra's child; but Attalos, knowing Alexander, decided to take no risks, and sent Alexander Demosthenes' letter. Alexander had neither forgotten nor forgiven, but Attalos had a certain reputation and following ... It might be better to let him alone for the present.

So serious was the situation that Alexander's counsellors advised him to abandon Greece for the present, and try by negotiation to avert a general revolt in Thrace and Illyria.

But this was not Alexander's way.

He had, naturally, already made diplomatic speeches to the deputations from Greek states which had attended Philip's last festival at Aigai. Greece was now to see him in action.

It is at this point that there begins the best of the ancient sources for Alexander's reign : the military narrative of Arrian, a Greek who himself held military commands under the Roman Empire, and who based his narrative on the memoirs of two of Alexander's officers, the engineer Aristoboulos and Ptolemy, later King of Egypt.

Long before his opponents could concert any action, Alexander was in Thessaly with his army. The horse-riding squires – the class which had gained by Philip's overthrow of a dictatorship based on mercantile Pherai and its port – welcomed him with enthusiasm, and cheered his references to 'our common ancestors, Achilles and Hêrakles'. But he could not stay long there. Demosthenes was still endeavouring to organize resistance, and referring to him as 'that boy'.

By forced marches the army pushed on southwards, through Thermopylæ, through Phokis; in Boiotia more news came in. Alexander's speed had made an impression; the nationalists were losing ground. But the irreconcilable Demosthenes was still struggling, and referring to Alexander as 'that stripling'.

'They'll find I'm grown up under the walls of Athens,' said Alexander.

But before they came near Athens all was decided – bloodlessly, for the moment. The anti-Macedonian movement collapsed, the peace parties in the cities regained control. By the autumn, Alexander had secured from a new session of the League at Corinth the recognition of his position as Captain-General of the League with the charge of conducting the war of revenge against Persia.

At Corinth the chief celebrities of Greece came to salute the young King. But one resident there, of whom Alexander heard much talk, did not come: the philosopher Diogenes, known as the Cynic – 'the Dog-Man' – a caustic and forcible preacher against the vanities of the world, who, though he might have had all the material advantages that a popular preacher could ask for, preferred to live in a tipped-up clay storage jar on a piece of waste land, with a minimum regard for decency, cleanliness or comfort. It was with him, in fact, that the Cynic movement, founded long since by a disciple of Sokrates, first became a social force, in reaction against an age of vulgarity and the love of riches. Its ascetic preachers, the mendicant friars of their day, were soon to be well known.

In the end, Alexander decided to call on Diogenes.

The story of their interview belongs to a cycle of anecdotes about Alexander's magnanimity towards people who stood up to him; but it is at least in character, on both sides.

Diogenes lay in the sun among the dust and stones, made no move to get up, showed no sign of being impressed by the King's brilliant suite and no particular desire for conversation. Alexander finally asked, 'Is there anything I can do for you?'

'You and your friends can stop keeping the sun off me,' said Diogenes.

It is in accordance with all we know of him if Alexander recognized in the ascetic something that he knew in himself also : the passion to drive one's self to the uttermost, the determination to be beaten by no difficulty and no privation, and to admit the superiority of no man.

'Upon my word,' he said as they walked away, 'if I were not Alexander, I would be Diogenes.'

Back in Macedonia that winter, preparing to settle accounts in Thrace and Illyria, Alexander decided to get rid of Attalos. It is not clear whether, since handing over Demosthenes' letter, Attalos had done anything more compromising; but since the day of Cleopatra's wedding, Alexander had regarded him as an enemy.

High Macedonian officers could not be simply relieved of their commands. Such a step would have been regarded by any Macedonian nobleman as probably the prelude to arrest, and certainly a ground for rebellion or desertion. Now or earlier, therefore, an agent appropriately named Hekataios, from Hekate, the queen of Hell, was sent to Parmenion's army in the Tröad with the secret mission of compassing Attalos' death.

There remained the north Balkans.

As soon as the snow was off the passes in the year 335, Alexander marched for Thrace; eastward to Amphipolis, past Philippi, past Neapolis (Kavalla), and then inland over the Rhodope mountains to Philippopolis. Thus far, thanks to his father's fortresses, roads and colonies, he was in friendly territory; but now the Thracians, stiffened by some armoured infantry – Greek traders resident in their country – were gathered to dispute his passage of the Shipka Pass, over the main Balkan range.

It is striking to see how Alexander, in this his first major campaign, shows all the complete self-confidence, resourcefulness, dash and leadership that he showed on later and more famous fields. There is no trace of development in Alexander's generalship; in his twenty-first year of his age he is completely mature. He stormed the spur west of the Shipka at the head of his light infantry, while his archers galled the defence from a spur on the opposite flank; and between the two his phalanx scrambled grimly up the pass. The Thracians had a stratagem ready : they had collected hundreds of waggons, which they were ready to send flying down the hill into the crowded ranks. Then they would follow with the dreaded Thracian broad-sword charge. But Alexander had got wind of the plan and given orders accordingly. They were, where possible, to open ranks and let the wagons through; and where rough ground made this impossible, to crouch prone, with their serried shields held over their heads like a roof. Macedonian drill and discipline were good; and as Alexander had foreseen, the wagons – light vehicles built for mountain country – ran up over the roofs of shields and crashed harmlessly in rear. There were a few broken bones, but not a single màn was killed. The Macedonians, tremendously relieved and somewhat surprised at finding themselves unhurt, went forward again with a triumphant roar; the light-armed troops poured in their missiles from both flanks, and, almost without striking a blow, the Thracians fled.

Alexander marched on to the Danube, defeating en route the fierce Triballoi, who had given his father more than one hard fight. There he met his fleet, partly supplied by the Greeks of Byzantium, apparently at a prearranged rendezvous : striking evidence of the accurate geographical knowledge at his disposal. He even crossed the great river, ferrying over 4,000 infantry and 1,500 cavalry, secretly and in a single night, with his ships, local dug-out canoes and rafts made of the army's leather bivouac tents, rolled up and stuffed with chaff (for the region was under corn), and at dawn surprised and routed a large force of the half-Scythian Getai, who had gathered to dispute his crossing. It was a sound move, to give the Getai this demonstration of his power; but one of Alexander's chief motives is said to have been simply the feeling that anyhow he *wanted to go* beyond the Danube; an example of that outlook on all life as a glorious adventure and that Odyssean desire to see and know, which remained characteristic of him all his days.

On the Danube he dictated peace to the King of the Triballoi and received deputations from the remoter tribes up the river, most picturesque among whom were the Gauls: big, loose-jointed, red-, brown- or golden-haired men newly migrant from central Europe. With them he swore peace and alliance – they might be useful in giving the Illyrians something else to think about, when Alexander should be gone into Asia. He asked them what in the world they most feared, hoping for a diplomatic answer; but the Gauls looked about them and said that they were a little afraid that the sky might fall one day ... They had probably just been swearing friendship in the terms of the old Keltic oath, binding 'until the sky fall, or the sea rise and cover us, or the earth open and swallow us up'.

Alexander laughed, and let the matter drop.

His halt on the Danube was ended by serious news: Kleitos, son of Philip's old enemy Bardylis, King of Illyria, was gathering his hill-men in the mountains south of Lake Ochrid. It was no more than might have been expected; but there was no time to be lost, for Kleitos was only eighty miles west of Pella, while Alexander was two hundred miles north-east of it. Moreover, a tribe en route, the Autariatai, were to prevent Alexander from intervening by harassing his march. Here, however, an ally came to the rescue: Langaros, King of the warlike Agriânes, old allies of Philip against their neighbours the brutish Triballoi.

'Don't worry,' said Langaros gaily; 'the Autariatai are the feeblest fighters in the whole land, and I and my people will give them plenty to think about.'

So the army that Philip had trained to march thirty-three miles in a day with full armour and several days' flour swept from the Danube south-westward; and before Kleitos' allies from the Adriatic had arrived, Alexander was before him, sweeping him from the hill positions, from which he had hoped to fall on the Macedonians' flanks as they passed, back into his walled town of Pelion. As the Macedonians advanced, they passed a newly made altar, by which lay the bodies of three youths, three maidens and three black rams, sacrificed by the Illyrians to their hungry gods ... The advance had been so rapid that they had not had time to complete the ceremony.

Next day came difficulties. While Alexander lay before the walls, Glaukias, King of the Taulantioi (in northern Albania), arrived with a horde of his tribesmen, horse and foot, and occupied the mountains in his rear. For once the Macedonians (only just arrived in the vicinity) had been caught napping. The baggage beasts of the army, grazing in the water-meadows upstream, had to be rescued by Alexander with the whole of his light infantry; and even after that the enemy felt that, camped in a meadow with a river and an enemy fortress on one side of him, mountains held by the enemy on the other, and foothills, descending to the river, dominating the ford on his line of retreat, the King of Macedonia was in a trap.

Alexander's method of extricating himself was as original as usual. He paraded his phalanx in mass, 120 ranks deep, with cavalry on the flanks, and proceeded to give a display of drill for the benefit of the enemy. Up and down, right and left, the great hedgehog of spearmen moved, marching, turning and halting with disciplined precision, while Glaukias' men, who had never seen anything like it, looked down from the hills round-eyed with astonishment. Then, when he judged that a sufficient impression had been created, Alexander suddenly set the whole mass in motion towards the enemy on the foothills.

The sight of twelve thousand pikes approaching in grim silence at a ponderous double-march was too much for undisciplined men. Those on the lowest spurs fled, without waiting for a nearer view, running all the faster when, at the word of command, the whole Macedonian army broke silence with the battle-yell 'Alalalalai!' and the deafening clang of spears beaten against their shields. Alexander shouted to his personal guard to mount and follow, and dashed to seize the spur overlooking the ford.

Once there, he ordered up in support his archers, 2,000 strong, and his mountain troops, 1,000 Agriânes, old allies, hired by Philip long ago; while his regular light infantry, followed by

the phalanx and the rest of the army, splashed through the
river out of the enemy's ring.

The position of the rearguard was still ticklish, for the tribesmen, seeing the Macedonians retreating, began to close again;
but when the rearguard charged boldly, while the phalanx on
the far bank shouted again and made as if to recross, they
hastily drew back. The rearguard then crossed in turn, the last
of them covered by archers (whom Alexander, crossing with
them, though slightly wounded in the head by a slingstone, had
halted in the river bed after passing midstream) and by 'field
artillery' : portable catapult-engines, shooting stones and heavy
javelins at their extreme range of several hundred yards – another disconcerting surprise. The Illyrians wavered again, and
the last of the rearguard slipped beyond their reach.

Alexander had not lost a man in the whole operation.

Two days later, scouts brought word that the tribesmen,
thinking they had their enemy on the run, were encamping
without precautions. Alexander recrossed the river a little
distance away, by night, leading his light division, with the
heavy infantry following; but, personal reconnaissance con-
firming what the scouts had said, he decided not to wait for
them. At dawn the archers and Agriânes burst into one end of
the great disorderly camp, strewn at excessive length along the
valley; killing Illyrians sleeping, rising or running; the other
light infantry following in a long, cheering line. The camp was
swept from end to end; there was no resistance, and a long and
grim pursuit. 'Those who escaped,' says Arrian, 'escaped without their arms.' King Kleitos fell back into the city again, burnt
it and fled with Glaukias.

It was not yet a week since Alexander had arrived before
Pelion.

Once more speed had saved a dangerous situation; for at
Pelion news reached him that two Macedonian officers had been
murdered in the streets of Thebes, and that the people had
risen and were besieging his garrison in the citadel.

The disappearance of a Macedonian king and his army into the hinterland had given rise, not for the first time in a

country much given to wishful thinking, to the rumour that he was dead – killed by the Illyrians, said the Thebans; by the Triballoi, said Demosthenes, who produced a wounded man who claimed to have received his wound in the same battle. Moreover, Persian gold was being pumped into Greece in a steady stream. Athens had not moved yet, but the war party had privately supplied arms and money to the insurgents at Thebes. Sparta had always refused to sign the convention of Corinth. Arcadia was moving. The Greek question would have to be settled in no uncertain fashion, or there could be no march into Asia.

The victorious army swung southward along one of the Pindos valleys that run conveniently for one travelling from north-west to south-east, probably that of the upper Haliakmon; over the saddle north of Aiginion (Kalabaka); and so, unheralded, to Pellina in western Thessaly, on the seventh day from Pelion. Sixteen miles a day for a week with armour and baggage, along rough mountain tracks, was good going; but there was no halt at Pellina, and with easier country their speed rose to twenty miles a day. By the time news reached Thebes that the Macedonian army had passed Thermopylæ, Alexander was encamped at Onchestos, one day's march away.

The Theban leaders could not believe their ears. Alexander was dead; it must be the Macedonian home army under Antipatros; or perhaps Alexander the Lynkestian.

But on the thirteenth evening from Pelion, Thebes knew that the camp-fires before its walls were those of the Macedonian main army under Alexander son of Philip. They had marched 240 miles in thirteen days and were ready for immediate battle. Alexander, anxious to conciliate Greece, waited one night, to see if this would bring Thebes to reason; but too many Thebans had too much to lose. The reply was a sortie of cavalry and light troops right up to his lines, which inflicted some casualties before being driven back. Alexander then marched round the city on to the Athens road, where he could be seen by his men in the citadel, and delivered his ultimatum: demanding the surrender of certain named irreconcilables to be dealt with at his discretion. There was a collaborationist party in Thebes, and there was fierce debate; but the war party prevailed, and the reply sent was an ironical demand for the surrender of Antipatros and Philôtas, the commander of Alexander's horse-guards. Alexander deployed his army for an assault.

Even now he did not yet give the order to attack; but battle was joined apparently (according to Ptolemy) as the result of a piece of feudal indiscipline that would never have taken place in his later campaigns.

The wall of the citadel, held by Alexander's garrison, was, on the south side, the wall of the town. The Thebans had cut it off from the outside world by a double line of entrenchments, with ditches and palisades, and against this less formidable obstacle the second battalion of the phalanx, mountaineers of Orestis in western Macedonia, with their hereditary chief Perdikkas as colonel, went forward, Perdikkas leading, in impetuous assault; broke through the palisade, and pressed on to take in rear the inner line facing the citadel. Amyntas, son of Andromenes, commanding the next battalion, seeing Perdikkas advancing unsupported, on his own initiative committed his 1,500 men in support; and Alexander, arriving on the scene, sent in the archers and the Agriânes, on his invariable practice of never committing heavy infantry alone. The rest he still held back, to see what would happen.

Perdikkas and his men pressed on, driving the defenders back through a gate of the town wall into the Hollow Way, a street running past the citadel into the centre of the town. But the Thebans were now rallying to the threatened point. Fighting became intense. Perdikkas fell wounded at the inner palisade, and a counter-attack from the Hollow Way sent Alexander's archers flying, with seventy men killed, including their commander. Things looked ugly; yet it was at this very moment that Alexander snatched victory out of a planless, stupid, mêlée. His quick eye saw the counter-attackers getting out of hand in pursuit, and he chose this moment to launch the main army in support of the attack.

Back again, the tide surged inwards along the Hollow Way; but this time there was a far greater press of bodies. The mob of Thebans, struggling to get through the gate, prevented it being shut. The Macedonians pressed through it along with them; mounted the wall, which was not manned, having been covered by the palisade; joined hands with the garrison of the citadel, and promptly delivered an attack through the gates on the opposite side of the citadel into the heart of the town.

That was the end. A formed body of Thebans still fought round the Temple of Amphîon; but not for long. And then, says Arrian, it was not so much the Macedonians but the neighbours of Thebes, whose cities Thebes had sacked in the days of her power and arrogance, who now 'slaughtered the Thebans indiscriminately, some in the houses where they took refuge, some turning at bay, some even in the temples, sparing neither age nor sex'.

This looks like an attempt to whitewash Alexander's own troops, among whom at least his barbarian auxiliaries were not backward in pillage. That evening a Theban lady who had been raped by a Thracian captain was brought before him; not to make her complaint, but to be charged with murder by the Thracian's comrades. The Thracian had demanded with menaces where she had hidden her valuables. She had answered, in the well in the garden. There she had led him, and when he was looking down it, pushed him in and pushed the parapet on top of him.

Alexander interrogated her. Her name was Tîmokleia, she said; sister to the general Theâgenes who had fallen at Chaironeia; also (it appears) newly widowed. She was evidently a woman of breeding, spirit and courage. Alexander acquitted her of all blame, sent the disgusted Thracians away and let her depart freely with her children.

But while he might gratify his sense of chivalry by turning one woman loose on the road, Alexander seems to have felt that an example must be made of Thebes to impress Greek opinion. Only so can we explain the fact that he then called a conference of the Greek allies – in practice, a court of the same old enemies of Thebes – to decide what should be done with the rebel city, now, as in the days of Xerxes (said the prosecution), taking the side of Persia against united Greece. The result was a foregone conclusion. Thebes was to be razed. Temples with their priests, and the house of Pindar with the descendants of the great poet, were spared; and collaborators and friends of the Macedonians were set free. But for the rest, the city was systematically destroyed, its territory distributed among its neighbours, and the whole citizen population sold as slaves. They numbered some 30,000, mostly women and children. Six thousand, mostly men, had perished in the battle and sack.

Greece was certainly impressed; in fact, shocked. Cities had been destroyed before now, but farther away, as in Sicily by the Carthaginians, or in the north by Philip; or much smaller cities, such as Melos by Athens or Plataia by Thebes – and even these deeds had left a stain on the reputation of the perpetrators. Shocked amazement certainly stilled all murmurs of revolt; and Alexander was able again to bid for the reputation of being a friend of culture by treating Athens with studied leniency. He demanded the surrender of Demosthenes and others, who had been implicated in the revolt at Thebes; but even these he permitted to be begged off by the pro-Macedonian Dêmades. He only insisted that the ruffianly *condottiere* Charidêmos (whom even Demosthenes could not stomach) must be banished; and Charidêmos went to Asia to join the group of Greek officers in the service of Persia.

Nevertheless, the destruction of Thebes seems to have left a certain uneasiness even in the conscience of Alexander. Sometimes he would attribute any misfortune to the anger of the Theban god Dionysos; and he was noticeably gentle to any Theban survivors whom he came across in later years.

With the autumn, Alexander was back in Macedon, having packed into one summer marches and victories that might well have occupied a good general, with the same army, for three. Moreover, if the Greek campaign had been postponed for two years, it would certainly not have been finished in one year more.

News from the Asiatic front was chequered.

Hekataios had carried out his mission; Attalos was dead. Parmenion meanwhile had been having a difficult time. There was no hope of support from Macedonia this year, and the morale of his troops was not improved by the necessity of making away with his second-in-command. Moreover, his other corps commander, Amyntas the son of Antiochos, took fright and deserted to the Persians.

In these circumstances Memnon of Rhodes had been able to take the offensive, forcing Parmenion to abandon the siege of a town in the Tröad, and defeating a force under Kallas, the brother or cousin of Harpalos. But he had failed to retake Kyzikos, and Parmenion could congratulate himself on having held the essential bridgehead.

At home, once Attalos was out of the way, a number of his kinsmen were arrested and put to death. The slaughter of relatives, when anyone was put to death for 'reasons of state', was customary in Macedonia, lest they might take up the blood feud. At the same time, in Alexander's absence, Olympias had had her way with her younger rival, arresting her, killing her infant and roasting Cleopatra alive over a charcoal brazier – or, according to a less sensational story, merely forcing her to hang herself.

Alexander is reported to have considered this piece of barbarism unduly harsh. But that he should take any action against his adored but terrible mother seems to have been for him unthinkable.

The chief work of this winter was, however, financial.

It is not often appreciated that Philip, for all his victories and his new and productive gold mines, died leaving a deficit: a debt, that is, of 500 talents or 3,000,000 drachmas (a drachma being the usual maximum daily wage of a skilled workman or highly trained soldier); a sum equivalent to the cost of a summer's campaign, and a formidable burden in a world both unmechanized and unacquainted with the blessings of banking. That this should have been the position at the end of Philip's highly successful reign shows how expensive his army – especially its large professional ('mercenary') component – was, and how, like some greater and more recent militarist powers, the new Macedonia had to go on in its career of aggression or collapse; i.e. revert to smallness in a world full of enemies. *Retrenchment to a level which could be covered by the resources of Macedonia meant breaking up Philip's army*. Naturally, Alexander never for a moment considered such a course; and this was one more reason, and the most insistent, if not the most congenial to Alexander, for pressing on with the Great Adventure.

· Alexander was not at all dismayed by the financial position. He was perfectly confident that he was going to conquer Persia and, to raise the necessary working capital, he proceeded without a tremor to increase the debt from 500 talents to 1,300. As to where he raised the money, we have no information; most of the rich men of Athens and the rest of mercantile Greece were at least lukewarm towards him. It seems probable on the whole that he raised his 800 talents chiefly from his own henchmen, the nobles of Macedon whom Philip had enriched, and that this is to be connected with the large-scale alienation of crown lands which he is also reported to have carried through at this time. Alexander is represented, it is true, as giving away these lands in an orgy of largesse; but, as this was a moment when he needed money particularly badly, it may be presumed that there was a *quid pro quo*. The financial dealings of Homeric chieftains naturally had their own etiquette; and when Perdikkas, descendant of the kings of Orestis, gave a lead to many other Companions, in gratefully declining the estate thrust upon him, one may assume that he put down his share of the cost of the venture without pressing his friend and King for security.

It is likely enough that when all was done, the crown lands alienated, and every available talent borrowed as well, Alexander replied, as the tale says, to the Companions who asked what he had left for himself with the superb 'conceit':

'My hopes!'

Even so, Antipatros and Parmenion were still dubious about the advisability of his plunging into Asia at once, especially since there was now no heir to the throne. Alexander, they knew, would insist on leading assaults and on reconnoitring personally; and one unlucky arrow might at almost any time plunge the whole kingdom back into the chaos of which it had such bitter experience. At least, they urged, let the King first marry and beget a son.

Alexander – it is characteristic of his psychology – would have none of it. It was now that he asked, was it a time for the King of Macedon to be dallying with women, when there was such great work to do?

More soberly, one cannot but reflect that this is the most crushing evidence of Alexander's irresponsibility. His ideals were purely self-centred. It gave him pleasure and served his great purpose – fame – to be munificent to his friends, attentive to his wounded, generous on occasion to a brave and attractive enemy; but his lifelong lack of interest in the succession, especially in view of his own recklessness, shows an utter carelessness of what happened to Asia, Greece or Macedon once he was gone.

5   Army and Leader

(Asia Minor, 334)

In the spring of the year 334, leaving all enemies at home dead or morally paralysed, Alexander marched for the Dardanelles. Twelve thousand infantry and 1,500 cavalry were left with Antipatros. The 240 miles were covered in twenty days, and while Parmenion superintended the ferrying of the main army across the Narrows, Alexander, himself steering his flagship, sailed down to Troy and sacrificed elaborately to the gods and to the possibly jealous ghosts of the mighty dead; dedicating his shield to Athêne and taking from her temple one said to have been that of Achilles; running naked round the tomb of Achilles and crowning it with a garland, while his bosomfriend Hêphaistion crowned that of Achilles' friend Patroklos.

'O fortunate Achilles,' said Alexander, 'who had Homer to praise him!'

From Troy he rejoined the army at Abydos. It is time for us to make the more detailed acquaintance of his host, which was to be the instrument of Alexander's fame and artistry and, for the rest of his life, his moving home.

It numbered something under 40,000 men all told, including over 5,000 cavalry – a high proportion by Greek standards. Of the infantry, some 13,000 were Macedonians, 12,000 Greeks and 7,000 barbarian allies; of the cavalry, some 1,800 were Macedonians, 1,800 Thessalians, 600 other Greeks and the rest Paiones and Odrysians (the great horse-riding tribe of Thrace).

It was a carefully balanced force.

Core and backbone of it was the famous phalanx, armed with the long sarissa; 9,000 strong, organized in six battalions of 1,500, territorially recruited. The men came chiefly from the mountain valleys of western Macedonia: the three battalions on which we have any information (the first, second and fourth in the usual battle-order) all bear the names of mountain regions. It looks as if the farmer-citizen-soldiers of old Macedonia were deliberately left for home defence, while the manpower of the recently conquered regions was taken abroad. Perdikkas, son of the last feudal lord of Orestis, commanded his own tribesmen and the men of Lynkestis, in the second battalion; retaining, it seems, a dash of feudal indiscipline which Alexander, knowing a good unit, did not suppress too heavily. Harpalos no doubt could have had the first battalion, which came from his forefathers' kingdom of Elymiotis; but he was physically unfit, and the command went to Koinos, son of Polemokrates, a grim soldier who served the King and had no further ambitions. The third battalion was under Amyntas, son of Andromenes, brave, honest and outspoken; the fourth under Ptolemaios, son of Seleukos (not the famous Ptolemy), the fifth under Meleagros, and the sixth under Krateros, ultimately the most trusted of all Alexander's marshals, and often left in charge of the main body when the King went off with a light column. In battle, Krateros commanded the left half of the phalanx and Koinos the right. He also was one of the chief marshals, being much used in command of offensive battle-groups. Koinos' and Krateros' respective roles corresponded to the positions of their battalions in line, for the first battalion in column always came to the right of the line, while those behind came up on its left.

The phalanx, being designed exclusively for pitched battles, actually did relatively little fighting, and at first came in for a good deal of inter-regimental badinage from the hard-worked light infantry. But in action or not, its influence was all-pervading, as providing the solid but movable base from which the light troops operated; not unlike the influence which the rooks in a game of chess may exert from the rear.

Phalanxes of spearmen – even Philip's – were particularly vulnerable to attack on the right flank, the shieldless side; and for this reason, Philip had developed a *corps d'élite* 3,000 strong, the three battalions of the Hypaspistai, who covered the right of the phalanx just as the hypaspistes ('shield-bearer' or 'squire') had covered the flank of the armoured chieftain in earlier barbaric warfare. These, especially their first battalion, the *Agêma*, were the footguards of the army, known later, at the end of Alexander's life, as the Silver Shields. They were 'medium infantry', well enough armoured to charge with the phalanx in battle, and also light enough for skirmishing or mountain warfare. Of all the Macedonian units, they were the most continuously employed.

Other heavy infantry formed a large proportion of the 12,000 Greeks (5,000 mercenaries and 7,000 citizen troops from the states of the Corinthian League). Alexander, however, used his League infantry chiefly as line-of-communication troops. As such they were useful; also they gave colour to Alexander's propaganda in Greece on the theme of the 'national crusade'; but what Greece really felt about it is shown by the fact that as many Greeks *fought* for Dareios as *served* on Alexander's side.

There were two battalions of archers – one of Macedonians, the other of Cretan mercenaries. In Europe last year they had totalled 2,000, but some may have been left with Antipatros. Lastly, light javelin-throwers, the typical skirmishing troops of Greek armies, were furnished by the Thracian and Illyrian allies. These (like the Greeks) also served as hostages for their relations at home.

One unit among these requires special mention: the 1,000 Agriânes. It must have required constant drafts to keep them up to strength. They were in every flying-column that Alexander ever led, and played an important part in his pitched battles as well. Furnished originally by Philip's old ally King Langaros, they were the Gurkhas of Alexander's army. We do not know the name of a single individual among them. They never mutinied, never grumbled (at least we never hear of it) and never let him down.

Among the cavalry, the 1,800 (later 2,000) Companions took the leading place. This famous regiment had developed out of the old Macedonian armoured chivalry, 600 strong at the beginning of Philip's reign, recruited from the *petite noblesse* of the Macedonian plain, and with a tradition of shock tactics already mentioned by Thucydides. Philip, having annexed the peninsula of Chalkidike, had later incorporated the cavalry forces of this region, both Greek and native, bringing the number of his squadrons up to eight. The Companions also included a considerable sprinkling of Greek soldiers of fortune who had risen in Philip's service and been rewarded by him with grants of land in his enlarged Macedonia that were the envy of Greece.

Nearly as important were the Thessalian cavalry: huntsmen and serf-owners, sons of rustic aristocrats like the Macedonian Companions themselves. The other Greek cavalry, though few at first, did good service in battle, causing Alexander to recruit more of them later. Lastly, two hard-working light cavalry regiments, much used in advanced-guard work, were the Paiones, from the borders of Macedonia, under a fierce head-hunting chieftain of their own, named Ariston, and the Thracian Prodromoi, or 'Fore-runners', i.e. Reconnaissance Regiment. The two units together were known as the Lancers (all the cavalry used lances, but these carried a particularly long weapon like the infantry sarissa); and both, sometimes, are called Prodromoi.

The sea-crossing was covered by 160 war-galleys, mostly supplied by Athens and the other sea-powers of the League. Persia could raise, chiefly from Phœnicia and Cyprus, a fleet superior both in quality and numbers; but having gone home for the winter, it arrived too late to interfere.

Alexander's officers were partly his personal friends – especially the group whom Philip had once exiled – and partly Philip's men; all of them truly 'the King's Companions' in the traditional phrase. Parmenion, whom Philip once called 'the only general he had ever met', was the chief military expert; but he was not 'chief of staff' as it comes so naturally to us to say. Alexander was his own chief of staff. In the three great pitched battles, Parmenion commanded the left or defensive

wing, while Alexander attacked on the right – characteristically reversing the roles of Collingwood and Nelson.

Alexander's two chief assistants with his ever-increasing
correspondence were his lifelong friend and confidant Hêphaistion, and the Greek secretary Eumenes, whom Philip had found
young and obscure at Kardia on the Sea of Marmara, and trained
into the indispensable head of his 'chancery'. As business increased, inevitably Hêphaistion found himself charged with
more official work, and Eumenes with increasing responsibility,
and some friction developed between them. Harpalos, unfit for
soldiering, became Lord Treasurer, while his cousin Kallas commanded the Thessalian horse. The grizzled Erigyios of Mytilene
commanded the other Greek cavalry, while his brother Laomedon, who spoke Persian, was in charge of prison-of-war administration, and several times produced valuable intelligence.
Ptolemy, rather later, appears as a sort of intelligence and
security officer, to whom men reported the discovery now of a
conspiracy and now of an oil-well. Kallisthenes, the nephew of
Aristotle, was chief scientific observer and official historian
and also, as the court philosopher, was expected to advise on
points of casuistry or morals; and there were several other
Greek historians and poets, forming in effect a kind of Propaganda Department.

Personal services and minor staff duties – anything from
carrying Alexander's helmet to taking messages and dealing
with visitors – were carried out by the royal pages, who also
guarded the King's quarters at night. There were some scores of
these young gentlemen, all sons of Macedonian landowners or
others of the King's friends. Philip had introduced the service,
through which young nobles were introduced early to military
and civil administration, and incidentally served as hostages.
When opportunity offered, Kallisthenes looked after their education; and in the minds of some, the theories of Greek philosophy were in the end to clash with the facts of military
absolute monarchy, with tragic results.

The commanders of the socially less regarded light and technical troops were career soldiers, like Diades of Thessaly, the

chief siege-engineer, who won fame at Tyre; but among the Companions, every man was a potential officer. In battle, Alexander charged surrounded by old friends: Hêphaistion, 'Black' Kleitos, the brother of his nurse, old Dêmarâtos of Corinth, who had once reconciled him to his father, and so on. Kleitos commanded the First or Royal Squadron of the Companions, while the whole brigade was under Philôtas, son of Parmenion. Nîkânor, the second son of Parmenion, commanded the Hypaspistai, next in the line, while Koinos, on the right of the phalanx, was their brother-in-law. (That family certainly seemed to have secured the 'strategic positions'.) Over on the left wing were Kallas and Krateros, under old Parmenion himself. Later a certain Kleandros, son of Polemokrates, and so probably brother of Koinos, appears as an important commander of mercenaries, and Alketas, brother of Perdikkas, as a phalanx colonel ... Never could an army so aptly have been described as a 'band of brothers'; but, like some brothers, they could quarrel even fratricidally.

Of the technical services we know only that they were efficient. The wounded were promptly cared for, and Alexander would personally visit his field hospitals after a battle. The siege-train, before a city in India, had its catapults in action on the first day, a wooden tower on wheels, over-topping the walls, on the second, and dropped a drawbridge from the tower on to the walls on the third. Walls too solid for the battering-ram were brought down by undermining. The largest rivers were bridged with boats, or crossed on rafts supported on the leather bivouac tents. The engineers also included a road-survey section, probably with measuring wheels, whose data added considerably to geographical knowledge.

Amenities for the troops were also Alexander's constant care. Home leave was granted to the newly married during the first winter, and in Egypt a Greek dramatic and concert party was brought over for the army's entertainment; while at every prolonged halt sports and musical and dramatic competitions were held for prizes awarded by Alexander.

From Abydos the army marched eastward ready for battle, the Lancers and a squadron of Companions reconnoitring ahead. It encountered the Persian army under Memnon and the satraps of Asia Minor holding the line of the Granikos torrent not far from the Sea of Marmara. Five thousand cavalry from Iran, Medes and Bactrians, were on their right, the satraps with their own heavy cavalry (at least another 5,000), on their left, where Alexander might be expected, and a strong corps of Greek mercenary infantry in the centre, with a cavalry screen in front of them along the river. This arrangement, which in effect failed to make use of the Greeks at all, looks so lunatic that it suggests that Memnon had doubts of their morale, unless Persians engaged first; but the satraps' plan was, as Tarn pointed out, not to hold the river-line – it was to kill Alexander.

Memnon indeed had strongly urged the Persians to avoid battle, harassing the invader with their swarms of cavalry, and burning the country, 'not sparing even the towns'. If Alexander could not live on the country, he would have to retire. But he came up against all that was most deep-seated in a Persian nobleman's view of his duty. Arsîtes, Satrap of Hellespontine Phrygia, probably commanding in chief because operations were taking place in his territory, spoke for his colleagues when he said, 'For my part, I will not voluntarily see one house burnt of the people who have been placed under my charge.' Some of the Persians, moreover, suspected Memnon of desiring to protract the campaign in order to make himself indispensable.

It was still early summer, and the river ran strongly, though generally fordable. Its bottom was stony, its far bank, swarming with mounted Persians, broken, but steep in places. Alexander's army approached in its usual battle order : Philôtas on the right with the Companions, covered by archers and Agriânes; then the lancers, Hypaspistai, phalanx, Thracian light infantry, Greek cavalry, with the Thessalians on the left wing. The two armies faced each other in a tense silence.

Parmenion proposed postponing the assault till the morrow; at first light, he said, the light infantry could seize beachheads before the Persians were ready, into which the heavy troops could cross and form up. But Alexander rejected the plan, on the ground that Persian morale would improve if their enemy hesitated to assault immediately. Parmenion mounted and rode off to his position on the left of the line, and the Persian leaders drew towards the point where Alexander was visible, conspicuous by his brilliant armour, his burnished steel helmet with a great white plume nodding on either side and the way in which those near him sprang to execute his commands.

Of the *mêlée* that followed, we have a spirited account, based on first-hand narratives, though differing in such details as precisely which Persian was killed by whom; an account which may serve as the best extant description of Alexander in battle.

Alexander sent in first the lancers, one battalion of Hypaspistai and the squadron of the Companions 'on duty' (the same which had been with the vanguard) against the Persian left centre, to 'fix' and hold the enemy.

A few moments later he himself mounted his charger – he did not risk Boukephalas that day – and with a shout of 'Now follow, and play the man!' rode down into the river, swinging out first to the right as though to reach the enemy's flank. The Companions followed majestically, with screaming of trumpets and the deep battle-cry invoking the God of War.

As the lancers drew near, the Persians received them with a hail of throwing-spears, 'some', says Arrian, 'from vantage points on the high banks, others meeting them at the water's edge. Horseman pushed against horseman on this side and on that, the Persians still showering their javelins, the Macedonians thrusting with their spears, but outnumbered and fighting at a great disadvantage from an unstable footing, and uphill out of the river bed ... Moreover the best of the Persian cavalry were here, and the sons of Memnon, and Memnon himself fighting in the front line. The first Macedonians to come to close quarters were killed to a man, fighting gallantly, except such as sheered off to join Alexander.

'For Alexander was now at hand, leading the right wing, and charged into the thickest of the Persian cavalry, where the Persian leaders were gathered; and round him there was severe fighting, while troop after troop of the Macedonians were crossing, now with greater ease. The battle, though waged on horseback, was more like an infantry fight; for they were wedged together, horse against horse and man against man, thrusting, the Macedonians to force the enemy back from the bank into the plain, and the Persians to deny them the landing and hurl them back into the river. But Alexander's men now began to reap the advantage of their strength and skill, and of the fact that they were fighting with cornel-wood lances against throwing-spears.

'Alexander's lance broke in the mêlée, and he called for another to Aretis, one of the royal grooms; but his was broken too, and he was giving a good account of himself with the broken piece, which he showed to Alexander and bade him ask somebody else. And Dêmarâtos of Corinth gave him his.'

The pressure must have relaxed for a moment, leaving Alexander and his Companions established on their hard-won footing. But the battle was not yet won. Spithridates, Satrap of Lydia, charged in furious counter-attack with forty kinsmen round him, and the other satraps followed.

'And Alexander with Dêmarâtos' spear, seeing Mithradates the son-in-law of Dareios spurring at him before the rest, at the head of a wedge of cavalry, charged out against him, and felled Mithradates, spearing him through the face. As he did so, Rhoisakes [the governor of Ionia] rode at him, and struck him on the head with his battle-axe, sheering off [the crest] from his helmet; but the helmet held . . . And Spithridates had got behind him with axe raised to strike, when Kleitos the son of Drôpides, in the nick of time, struck him on the shoulder, severing his arm.' At the same moment Rhoisakes fell, with Alexander's short sword through his breast. 'And all this time more and more cavalry were pouring across the river and joining Alexander.'

Meanwhile the battle seems to have been joined at other points, but there was little serious fighting. The Persians opposite Alexander gave way at last before the great lances that killed their horses and thrust men through the face, and before the light-armed foot-men now mingling with the Macedonian cavalry with deadly effect. The breakthrough, once made, widened swiftly as in a broken dam, and the whole Persian cavalry fled, leaving over a thousand dead on the field; while Alexander, fighting mad, fell with archers, cavalry and phalanx together upon the unsupported Greek mercenaries, and slew till, after a horrible carnage, in which Alexander had his horse killed under him, the last 2,000 of them were permitted to surrender.

It had been a black day for the Persian nobility. In addition to those mentioned above, Mithrobarzanes, Satrap of Cappadocia, had fallen, two other cavalry commanders, the Persian officer commanding the mercenaries, a grandson of the late King Artaxerxes, and a brother of the reigning Queen. Arsîtes of Phrygia (who as Commander-in-Chief had probably been on the right wing) escaped to Daskyleion, his capital, found it indefensible and, appalled at the disaster, for which he felt himself responsible, fell on his sword.

Alexander had lost twenty-five Companions killed, sixty other cavalry and thirty infantry, in addition to several hundred wounded. Families of the fallen Macedonians were granted relief from land-tax and personal service. Alexander spent the next day visiting his wounded, 'asking each man how he had been wounded and giving them a chance to boast of their deeds'; burying the dead, especially the Persian commanders; and ordering a war memorial, to be executed by the famous sculptor Lysippos, at Dion in Macedonia, with statues to represent the twenty-five fallen Companions. To Athens he sent, for dedication on the Acropolis, three hundred Persian suits of armour, with the inscription :

'Alexander, son of Philip, and the Hellenes, except the Spartans, from the barbarians of Asia.'

In the same spirit, he sent the 2,000 prisoners to labour in chains in Macedonia, as traitors taken in arms against the national crusade.

(Ionia to Issos, 334–3)

The disaster at the Granikos left Persia without a field army this side of Taurus, and was followed by a *dégringolade des forteresses*. Daskyleion was left open; the impregnable Sardis surrendered without a struggle. From its citadel Alexander issued a proclamation granting to the Lydian people freedom and the use of their ancient laws (within his empire, *bien entendu*). The Greek cities on the coast opened their gates joyfully, King Dareios' small garrisons evacuating them by sea. Ephesos had another revolution, and the leaders of the pro-Persian oligarchy were dragged out of sanctuary and lynched. Alexander, here and elsewhere, confirmed the new democratic governments (Persia had favoured oligarchies or local despots), but insisted on a general amnesty, 'feeling', says Arrian, 'that if the people were given its head, innocent as well as guilty would suffer, through private enmity or the desire for loot'. Milêtos, once queen of the Black Sea, where there was a larger garrison, was taken by storm, while Alexander's navy, under Nîkânor son of Parmenion, slipped into its harbour just before the superior enemy fleet arrived to relieve it.

Parmenion proposed to risk a sea battle, hoping that Greek courage might achieve the unexpected, and pointing out that, anyhow, as the Phœnicians were superior already, there was little to lose; but Alexander rejected the plan, not only from an ingrained habit of contradicting Parmenion, but on the ground that a defeat in the Ægean would spoil the moral effect of the initial victory and might have deplorable repercussions in Greece.

It is worth noticing that it was Parmenion on this occasion

who proposed the more dashing and risky plan, and that Alexander rejected it from his usual profound sense of the importance of moral factors; also that, while history records the occasions when Alexander, in his early twenties, rejected with complete success the old marshal's advice, the occasions when his advice was taken no doubt passed unremarked.

The case for forcing a decision at sea rested partly on financial grounds. The 160 galleys – triremes and the new quadriremes – needed at least 30,000 men. The treasury was still empty; to raise war contributions was always a sure way to cause disaffection in Ionia; and sailors, as a rule, had to buy their provisions in ports; they could not simply take them, or buy cheaply at the source, on the land.

Shortly afterwards Alexander solved this problem by metaphorically 'burning his boats', and sent his whole fleet home. Let the political position in Greece only be held over the winter, and he would settle with the Phœnicians by smoking out their nests ...

It remained to capture the main Persian base in the Ægean: Halikarnassos in Karia, where Memnon – now, too late, appointed by the King Supreme Commander in Asia Minor – had collected the garrisons from Ionia. Greek mercenaries and Karians under the Persian satrap Orontobates, and Macedonian exiles – among them a brother of one of Alexander's brigadiers – put up a vigorous defence, making repeated sorties to try to burn the rams, which from behind their great wooden shields were soon battering the walls. One night the town was very nearly taken by pure accident, when two drunks (from Perdikkas' battalion, one notes without surprise) 'dared' each other to go and storm a breach all by themselves; and proceeded to do so, killing the first few enemy who came near them, and engaging those who remained on top of the ruins with missiles. Others of their comrades ran up to join in, and a highly successful skirmish developed. Before a regular attack could be mounted, however, the besieged had 'sealed off' the breach with a half-moon inner wall of bricks, and the siege-engines moving up against it came under enfilading fire from the towers still standing. But the movement, the original wall having been breached on a 'three-tower' front, went relentlessly on; a final sortie ended in disaster to the besieged, and the loss of over 1,000 killed (Alexander also losing three senior officers); and that same night Memnon and Orontobates burnt their military stores and retired to the two formidable promontory-citadels. The town caught fire, and the Macedonians followed up through the blazing streets, doing what they could to help the Greek inhabitants.

Alexander, after one look at the two forts by daylight, decided that there was no need to assault them; he razed what was left of the town, left a brigade in Karia and marched to subdue the mountainous country eastward, having effectively 'liquidated' Halikarnassos as a base.

As Governor of Karia he left Queen Ada, the heir, widow and sister (according to local custom) of Idrieus, the late King. She had been deposed by that Prince Pixodar whose daughter Alexander had once thought of marrying. Alexander got on extremely well with Ada, addressing her as 'Mother'; while she fussed over him, hoping he was going to take plenty of warm clothes with him into the mountains, sending him sweets and savouries from her kitchen, and finally trying to give him several of the kitchen staff as a present. Alexander laughingly refused, saying that when he was a child his tutor Leonidas had taught him that the best appetizer for breakfast was a night march, and for dinner a light breakfast. 'Why,' he added, 'the man positively used to go through my clothing- and blanket-chests, to see whether my mother had slipped in anything luxurious or unnecessary.'

He finished off the year's operations with a swift and by any ordinary standards extremely tough campaign, reducing to obedience the mountaineers of Lykia and Pisidia, whom the Persian government had preferred to let alone, before turning north to Gordion, where the columns which had cleared north-west Asia Minor had their rendezvous for the winter.

While still in Pisidia he received serious news. Parmenion

in Phrygia sent him a captured Persian secret agent who under interrogation 'came clean'. His name was Asisines, sometime Ambassador in Macedonia, and his mission was from Nabarzanes, Dareios' Captain of the Guard and Chief Marshal to Alexander son of Aëropos. Dareios had received a message from the latter through the deserter Amyntas, asking, to put it crudely, how much Dareios would give to get rid of Alexander son of Philip. The answer was 1,000 talents, and every assistance in the task of securing the throne himself.

Alexander laid the matter before the Council of his Companions. He had trusted the son of Aëropos, and, in fact, had lately promoted him to the command of the powerful Thessalian cavalry, on the transfer of Kallas to a governorship ... The Council unanimously agreed that to trust the Lynkestian had been a mistake, and that he must be made harmless without delay.

Alexander decided that the matter was too delicate and dangerous for any written correspondence. He must send a senior officer with a verbal message ... Amphoteros, the brother of Krateros, crossed Asia Minor in peasant dress with a native escort; he slipped unnoticed into Parmenion's camp, and the traitor was placed under arrest.

Many a man had been killed for less, but so strong, apparently, was the following of the last Prince of Lynkestis, that his namesake did not venture to put him to death till years later. This, and still more the fact that Parmenion did not venture without orders to take any action at all, shows the strength of the survivals of feudalism in Macedonia even after Philip; one more factor, often unrecognized, among the difficulties over which Alexander triumphed.

At Gordion Alexander 'conceived a desire', as formerly to tread the northern bank of the Danube, so now to see the venerable farm-wagon of Gordieus, legendary ancestor of the old Phrygian kings called alternately Gordieus and Midas. Three hundred years after the fall of the kingdom, the old wagon which had been the embodied Luck of the rustic people (Aryan migrants?) was still preserved in the citadel; and a legend had

grown up round it. The ox-yoke and the pin which attached it
to the pole were secured by a knot of great complexity, with its
ends invisible; and the tradition ran, that he who could loose
the knot would reign over Asia. In that day, no doubt men
dreamed, God would at last restore the kingdom to Phrygia.

Whether Alexander knew of the tradition before he visited
the citadel does not appear; but, confronted with it, he did
some quick thinking. It would never do for him to depart
baffled ... He laid his hand, not on the cord, but on the pin;
pulled it out, and slid the yoke bodily out of the knot. Men
crowded round to see the secret of the Gordian knot; and not
two, but many rope-ends were seen. That night there was heavy
rain and thunder, and Alexander sacrificed to the sky-gods who
had thus approved his enterprise.

Such was the account of the matter given by Alexander's
officer Aristoboulos. That Alexander cheated in the grand manner by cutting the knot with his sword appears to have been
an early embellishment.

With the spring, the home-leave contingent of the newly
married came back, under the three newly-married colonels,
Koinos, Meleagros and Ptolemaios, son of Seleukos. With them
came drafts : 3,000 Macedonian infantry, 300 Macedonian and
350 Greek cavalry; much more than enough to set off all losses
hitherto. Strengthened and in good heart, the army marched out
via Ankara, on the road to Syria.

A native garrison held the formidable gorge through the
Taurus mountains, the Cilician Gates, where, until Ibrahim
Pasha blasted the rocks in the nineteenth century, there was
not room for two laden camels to pass. Alexander dashed ahead
to take them by surprise. He failed to do so, but the legend of
his invincibility, which his tremendous exploits had already
built up, had one of its greatest successes. At his mere approach
the defenders fled in a panic, and one of the strongest positions
in all Asia fell without a blow.

The army streamed down into the stifling plains at sea-level,
cut off from the north by the vast mountain wall; Alexander
still riding ahead with such as could keep up with him, in

answer to an appeal from Tarsus to come quickly, lest the retreating enemy might sack the town. Weary and with a fever
upon him after his exertions, he plunged into the Kydnos, cold
with the melting of the mountain snows. A few days later he
was seriously ill.

While he lay at Tarsus, tormented by fever and insomnia, he
received another 'most secret' message from Parmenion, whom
he had sent on with his Greek troops to seize the passes into
Syria. One of his doctors, Philip the Akarnanian, was said to
have been bribed to poison him. This was the more serious,
since Philip was the only doctor who was prescribing for him,
most of the others having fallen into a panic at the refusal of
the fever to yield to their treatment. Alexander, however, in
personal contact with Philip, felt intuitively that the accusation
was false. He waited till Philip came in with his medicine (a
strong purgative), took the cup from him, gave him the letter
and drank the medicine while he read it. Philip read it through,
and said quietly: 'You can trust me.' Shortly afterwards the
fever broke, and Alexander slept deeply for the first time for
days.

All this time the Persian fleet was still unopposed in the
Ægean. With it and his remaining Greek mercenaries, Memnon
did what he could against Alexander's communications with
Greece, re-occupying Chios and laying siege to Mytilene. Then,
a severe blow to Persia, he fell sick and died.

He left his command, subject to confirmation, to Pharnabazos and Autophradates, two Persians of great 'colonial' noble
houses, long domiciled in the west. Mytilene fell to them,
and then Tenedos, close to the Dardanelles. It became necessary
to remobilize the League fleets for the defence of Greece. The
trusty Amphoteros held the vital Straits, but Pharnabazos now
turned against the Cyclades; Agis, King of Sparta, too, was preparing to raise the standard of 'liberation' in the Peloponnese.
. . . The tension, however, relaxed somewhat when King Dareios'
orders to his new admirals (by the hand of Thymondas, nephew
of Memnon) confirmed them in their commands, but bade them

send back Thymondas, with all available Greek mercenaries, to join the main Persian army in Syria.

In Cilicia, Alexander also received news that his generals in Karia had routed and captured Orontobates. As a result the forts at Halikarnassos had fallen, with several neighbouring coast towns and the island of Kos. But the Persian fleet was still aggressive off the coast.

Consequently Alexander, when he recovered, still had to deal methodically with the coast towns of Cilicia, seeing that the local administration was in safe hands; and it was not till autumn that the army 'turned the corner' past the Syrian Gates and was moving south along the coast of the Levant. Beyond the mountains east of them, in the great plains of Syria, lay the main Persian army under the personal command of the Great King.

The last King of Persia was a distant cousin of his predecessor, elevated to the throne not long before Alexander's accession, by a palace intrigue; the late King, like *his* predecessor, having been made away with by his grand vizier, the eunuch Bagoas. Dareios was an imposing enough figure – tall and handsome, a blameless husband and father, a soldier, like all Persian noblemen. He had shown personal courage in his youth, killing an enemy champion in single combat during a local rising; he had governed Armenia and Media; and he showed a capacity for taking decisions when he promptly poisoned Bagoas, without waiting for Bagoas to poison him. But he was 'out of his class' as King of Persia against Alexander.

Philip's old enemy Charidêmos, arriving in exile at the court of Persia, had urged the King not to take the field in person. Given 100,000 men, of whom a third must be Greeks, he, Charidêmos, would finish Alexander's career in Asia.

Charidêmos had been making similar demands and offers, to Thracian chieftains or to the Athenian assembly, for the latter half of his life. Forgetting that he was not there now, he became so insolent in reply to those who advised His Majesty to take the field in person, that His Majesty lost patience and had him killed out of hand.

So the royal army lay in the plains of Syria. Its main strength was in cavalry: scale-armoured Medes and Persians, lighter-armed javelin-throwers, horse-archers of the nomad Sakai and Dahai from the borders of central Asia. The weak point was, as ever, the lack of good heavy infantry to stop and hold the enemy. The Persian staff had, however, done what it could: (a) by collecting all available Greeks including Memnon's land forces from the Ægean; and (b) by equipping and training Asiatics to fight in the Greek manner. Our authorities speak of 60,000 of these 'Kardakes', 30,000 Greeks, 600,000 Persian troops in all; all good round exaggerations. Twelve thousand Greeks, in fact, got away from the field of Issos, after a not unsuccessful battle on their part of the front; and the whole army was apparently small enough to pass a narrow defile in one night.

Through the hot summer the conscripted peasants sweated in Greek armour, learning to manœuvre – so far as might be – in mass and to handle the long pikes; and Dareios grew increasingly impatient under the strain of holding an army in deadly monotony, waiting for a foe who did not come. Alexander's delays, first through sickness and then in organizing the coast towns, steadily increased the Persian King's feeling that his enemy shrank from the decisive battle. 'Never fear,' said the exiled Amyntas. 'Stay here; Alexander will come to you, all in good time.' And for a space the King listened, keeping his post on the plains, where his swarms of horsemen could manœuvre, and which the enemy must traverse if he wished to march east.

When, however, Alexander at last emerged from Cilicia, and still did not come east, but south, Dareios could stand it no longer, and set his army in motion, down to the coast in Alexander's rear.

Alexander was marching on the Phœnician ports, still relentlessly carrying out his plan of eliminating the enemy's naval bases; a slow, sound, unhurrying plan; Alexander must this time have been in agreement with Parmenion. Phœnicia was an important objective, but not even for this had Alexander expected the enemy to entangle his great army among the mountains and in the narrow coastal plain. So certain was he, that he left a hospital, unprotected, at the town of Issos; the Persians overran it and 'blooded' their young barbarians by massacring and torturing the helpless sick.

It was late afternoon when news reached Alexander of enemy in force on the road behind him. He could hardly believe that it was the main Persian army, and sent back a fast cutter from his small inshore naval squadron to reconnoitre ... The officers aboard her reported that Dareios himself was at hand. They had seen all the shores of a bay, into which they had rowed, covered with horses and men, preparing to encamp, at the north end of the plain bisected by the Pinaros torrent. There was no sign of enemy troops nearer than that.

Alexander had meanwhile bidden his troops halt for supper, and sent a patrol back as far as the defile at the near end of the plain. He now addressed his officers, saying that this was the decisive hour; their past victories guaranteed success; all that was best in Greece was with them; and also – it is significant, already in this second year of the war – that this decisive battle would bring the end of their labours ...

Supper ended, the troops marched back in darkness by the way they had come. By midnight, the head of the main body reached the defile, where the coastal plain widened out. Having secured it, Alexander planted a strong outpost and bade the remainder of the army rest.

At first light he set the advance in motion again out into the plain, slowly and with precision. Lancers and Cretan archers were in front; then the pikemen, deploying from column into line as the front widened; then unit after unit of heavy cavalry, trotting forward into position on the flanks, filling up the gradually lengthening front from the mountains to the sea.

The first fighting took place on Alexander's right. The Persians had thrown forward troops along the hills to fall upon his flank; but the Agriânes and Macedonian archers made such short work of these irregulars that the only effective outflanking was done by them. Meanwhile Dareios, under cover of clouds of light horse and foot, had drawn up his main line behind the Pinaros torrent, fortifying the easier parts of its bank with a palisade of stakes: Greeks in the centre under Amyntas and Thymondas, in front of the King's huge chariot, a command-post on wheels; Oriental pikemen to right and left; cavalry massed on the seashore under Nabarzanes, the Captain of the Guard; and a strong force of archers at the base of the hills, where Alexander himself might be expected to charge. Alexander and his staff were quick to comment on the un-soundness, from the point of view of morale, of standing thus passively, waiting to be attacked; but the defence turned out not so passive after all.

Dareios' hopes of a decision, apart from the abortive effort of his mountain column, were to be based on a grand cavalry charge along the seaward flank. Most of the covering force withdrew to this flank, forming altogether such a formidable array that Alexander, who had hoped to mass all his best heavy cavalry on his own right, now detached the Thessalians to pass behind the phalanx, and reinforce Parmenion on the seashore; while the lancers, who had been skirmishing in front, dropped back into the line in their place. Thanks to Dareios' action in forcing a battle in so confined a space, many of his troops were piled up in rear unable to strike a blow, and even Alexander, with his smaller army, was able to hold back his Greek mercen-ary infantry, possibly mistrusting their behaviour should 'Greek meet Greek'.

By now the two armies were only a few hundred yards apart. Dareios high on his 'command vehicle', Alexander at the head of his horse-guards, were distinguishable from the opposing lines. The Macedonians advanced, still slowly and ponderously, with attention to the vital 'dressing' of the front rank. And then the first shower of Persian arrows burst upon Alexander's guards. Speed was now everything; Alexander set spurs to his horse, and the whole line, the right ahead of the left, went forward in full career. Simultaneously Nabarzanes' mailed horse-men swarmed over the torrent and thundered forward against Parmenion.

Parmenion was hard pressed; his leading squadron was rid-den over; but the Thessalians, more manœuvrable than the armoured Persians, hung on, making short, sharp, squadron charges, wheeling, supporting each other, and avoiding getting entangled with their heavy opponents. Meanwhile Alexander's charge, supported by the victorious Agriânes rushing down from the mountains, swept away the archers and laid bare the left flank of the Kardakes.

In the centre, the phalanx, mindful of the stinging jokes of other units about 'the Men Who Do Not Fight', charged grimly into the torrent bed and flung themselves at the steep bank and sharpened stakes beyond. It was a formidable obstacle. On their right they managed nevertheless to force it, against Kardakes who were inclined to look over their left shoulders to see what Alexander was doing. The left of the phalanx on the contrary, were brought to a standstill . . . The vital physical contact was lost between the two brigades, and Dareios' Greek mercenaries, seizing the opportunity, charged down the opposite bank of the torrent and into the gap.

Krateros' brigade was in a serious position : held from the front, threatened from the left, where a thin screen of javelin-men and archers formed the sole link with Parmenion's out-numbered horsemen, and now caught on an open right flank by the veteran mercenaries, eager to show that Greek pikemen could beat Macedonians. The fight took on the fierceness of a national duel. The fourth battalion, taken in front and flank, was severely handled; its colonel, Ptolemy, son of Seleukos, was killed, with 120 other Macedonians 'of name'; but his men – tough mountaineers from Tymphaia in the high Pindos – hung on grimly, and the mercenaries were not given time to complete their success. Alexander's victorious cavalry had turned in-wards; the left division of Kardakes, hard pressed in front by Koinos and Nîkânor, crumpled and gave way. The fighting came nearer and nearer to Dareios' great chariot, and the time came when any man in his army who had time to look towards the King could see (and tell his neighbour) that he was no longer there.

Then it was rout. The Asiatic infantry streamed to the rear. The mercenaries 'pulled out' just in time, not without loss in passing at the hands of Koinos' brigade, and took, unbroken, to the hills. Last of all, Nabarzanes' cavalry, baulked of their victory, rode off the field; but they were not to escape lightly. The narrow ways behind them were packed with fugitives. The Thessalians, after their struggle, had still *élan* for a murderous pursuit, and at every torrent crossing they had their revenge, killing and driving a disorganized enemy over the rocky banks till the dry gullies were blocked bank-high with a dam of horses and men.

Far ahead of these fugitives, Alexander and his Companions were pursuing Dareios himself. They had not been far apart when Dareios turned and fled; but the sheer press of men between was an obstacle, and there was no lack of Persian nobles and guardsmen ready to turn and die for the King. Nevertheless, they nearly had him at a wadi, where the unwieldy chariot stuck. But Dareios sprang down and was away in the nick of time on horseback, leaving his cloak and bow, and kept his distance till the early November nightfall covered his flight. Alexander, with an improvised bandage round a flesh-wound in the thigh, turned the Companions and rode back in darkness along the corpse-strewn road.

In the Persian camp his servants had made ready for him the royal tent of Dareios.

As he approached he heard the wailing of women from another great pavilion. It was the women of Dareios' family; the Great King's bow and cloak had been brought in, and his wife, mother and daughters were keening for the death of their lord. Alexander sent his Companion Leonnâtos to them to tell them that the King was alive, and bid them have no fear; they should receive every attention due to their position.

Next day he visited them, with Hêphaistion. Both were dressed alike, simply, in tunics and short riding cloaks, and the ladies in a passion of gratitude fell at the feet of Hêphaistion, the taller and statelier of the two. When aware of their mistake they were covered with confusion; but Alexander told them they had made no mistake at all; 'for he also is Alexander'.

Both contemporaries and later historians were surprised that

Alexander did not take Dareios' wife, a famous beauty, as his concubine. But now, as always, sex was of little interest and sensuality merely disgusting to him; and all he said, in answer to hints from his retinue, was that these beautiful Persian women were 'an irritation to the eyes'.

All he wanted that evening was food and rest. He limped into the royal tent; and there, under a blaze of torches, saw dinner spread out, not on his camp furniture, but with the gold plate and soft divans of the King of Persia. Alexander smiled.

'So this,' he said as he settled himself, 'is being a king!'

The glamour of the East was closing in on him; but he was still for the most part the Macedonian Prince who had read Homer as a boy and discussed the world with Aristotle. From the spoils, his friends presently brought him an exquisite jewelled casket 'suitable for the keeping of a king's greatest treasure'. Alexander was delighted, and used it as a travelling-box for his *Iliad*.

He was just twenty-three.

The Sacker of Cities

(Tyre and Gaza, 332)

Alexander resumed his march for Phœnicia.

Once more the main Persian field army had been crippled. Dareios, with about 4,000 Greek mercenaries, had vanished across the Euphrates; and Parmenion, with a cavalry column, seized unopposed the great magazines at Damascus and the royal war-chest, dispatched thither for safety some time before. The bullion taken was a small matter compared to the treasures which Alexander was to capture later, but enough to put an end to financial worries once and for all.

The cavalry also brought in a number of important prisoners; among others, ambassadors sent to Dareios from Athens, Sparta and Thebes. The Athenian was Iphikrates, son of Iphikrates the general. Alexander, ever anxious to placate Athens, kept him as a guest rather than a prisoner, 'out of his friendship for the city of Athens and out of regard for the achievements of his father', as was officially given out; also, probably, in the hope of finding his conversation interesting and instructive; and when he died, some time afterwards, sent his ashes home to his family. He also released forthwith the two Thebans; they were power-less to do any harm, and Alexander may still have felt qualms of conscience for his treatment of their city. Only the Spartan was kept, under open arrest, to be released only when Sparta also had been rendered impotent.

Shortly afterwards Dareios sent emissaries with a letter, to ransom the royal ladies, and to invite negotiations for peace.

Alexander replied in a letter of studied arrogance, evidently intended as a manifesto for public consumption. In answer to Dareios' complaints of his unprovoked attack, he raked up not only Persia's efforts to stir up trouble in Greece against Philip, but events dating back to the time of Xerxes; and, as the price of peace, he demanded unconditional surrender. He claimed the Empire as his by the arbitrament of battle, which was the decision of God. If Dareios wished for the return of his family, or anything else in reason, he should come personally and ask for it; or if he were afraid to do that, he might send some of his friends. Any further communications, however, should be addressed by Dareios, not as equal to equal, but humbly, as to the Lord of Asia from one of his subjects.

He sent an officer back with the envoys to deliver this letter, but strictly forbidden to enter into any negotiations.

Notwithstanding the tone he adopted to Dareios, Alexander was not without reasons for anxiety. It was now winter, the chill, rainy Syrian winter, and Persia was by no means beaten, even in the west. True, most of Phœnicia was surrendering: Arvad (Ruad island) with its extensive dependencies on the mainland; Byblos (Djebail); Sidon; but the mighty Tyre, Queen of the Levant, would go no farther than to propose neutrality. Alexander demanded at least a token entry into the island fortress to sacrifice in the Temple of Melkarth, whom Greeks identified with his ancestor Hêracles. The Tyrian nobles (their King Azramelech was with his fleet in the Ægean) replied politely that there was a temple on the mainland which would do just as well ... In mutual mistrust the negotiations broke down, and Alexander assembled his officers to explain exactly why Tyre must be taken, the Levant coast cleared and Dareios' communications with the Ægean cut, before it was possible to march on Babylon and Susa.

The news from the Ægean was, in fact, not good. Pharnabazos and Autophradates had recaptured Kos, and even descended unopposed upon Milêtos and Halikarnassos, though the Macedonian home fleet, reinforcing Amphoteros, had defeated an attempt to force the Dardanelles. The Persians now lay at Siphnos, one day's sail from the Greek mainland, with a hundred fast galleys, and Agis of Sparta had been over to confer with them. The conference had received a nasty interruption, in the news of the Battle of Issos; but both King and admirals were resolute men and were not deterred from sending Agis' brother, with ten ships and money for two months – all they could now spare – to stir up trouble in Crete.

Even the army which fought at Issos had been by no means annihilated; and Nabarzanes was reorganizing it in Armenia for an invasion of Asia Minor.

Also the enemy land forces, Ægean, were about to be reinforced. Eight thousand of Memnon's old mercenaries who had fought so stoutly at Issos, had broken away after the battle, under Amyntas and Thymondas, having in typical Greek fashion no wish to be cut off from home and the sea. They doubled back south through the mountains, reached Tripoli ahead of Alexander, seized the ships on which they had come from the Ægean and, having burnt the rest of the shipping, crossed over to Cyprus. Thence Amyntas attempted to secure Egypt, giving himself out to be the new Governor appointed by Dareios (the late Satrap had been killed at Issos). But neither natives nor Persian officials trusted him, and when Amyntas' troops tried to requisition provisions, disorders broke out and he was killed. Thymondas and the bulk of the mercenaries, however, went on from Cyprus to the Ægean and joined Agis, who felt that, thus reinforced, he could begin active operations.

This was the position which Alexander, so far as he knew it, outlined to his officers. Sparta was at war with Macedonia; Athens – he said candidly, however polite he might be to Athens in public – was kept quiet by fear rather than by goodwill. It was essential to prevent Persia from reinforcing the Ægean with ships and bullion. That was to say, they must take Tyre.

So in December the army started to build a mole, to fill up the sea between Tyre and the mainland.

At first all went well, but as the mole went forward, difficulties increased. The water was deepest near the island; catapults and archers on the towering walls picked off the men, unable to work in armour; and Tyrian galleys in unending relays enfiladed any forward cover from both flanks. The Macedonians wheeled forward two siege-towers to the end of the completed portion; massive structures of Lebanon cedar, bristling with catapults and marksmen, and covered from top to bottom with raw hides as a protection against incendiary missiles. They also ran rawhide screens along the whole length of the mole to protect the carrying-parties. But the Phœnicians were not at the end of their resources yet.

On a day of fresh west wind two powerful galleys approached the end of the mole, towing an extraordinary-looking craft, broad in the beam (she was, in fact, an old horse-transport) and with two slender masts right forward – in spite of which, her bows were high out of the water. From yard-arms on the two masts hung four large cauldrons, which smoked.

The Macedonians did not have long to look at her. One of the triremes swung to each side of the mole, the oarsmen rowing hard; and the fire-ship, her stern held down with ballast, crashed into the mole between the towers, riding over the planking for almost half her length. The two thin masts broke with the impact, the yards and their cauldrons fell, and a torrent of boiling pitch and oil poured out over the planks and burst into flame.

Half a dozen Phœnicians dived out of the fire-ship and swam home. The two galleys cast off the tow-ropes and poured in their arrows. Simultaneously a whole fleet of small boats dashed in to the attack; the Phœnicians landed all along the mole, tearing down its bulwarks, and set fire with incendiary materials to everything wooden, from the now blazing towers to the shore.

It was the darkest hour of the whole expedition. Tyre seemed impregnable, and meanwhile the Persian army from Armenia was marching to retake Asia Minor. There was deep depression in Alexander's camp, and the Council of the Companions was almost unanimous in favour of raising the siege. Could not Tyre, like the forts at Halikarnassos, be merely 'observed'? But Alexander, though tradition demanded that he should hear the Companions, did not take his decisions by a vote, and though only the stout-hearted Amyntas, son of Andromenes, supported him, the King would not tolerate the loss of prestige through a failure. He ordered the army to begin work on a new mole, much broader, to take more towers.

Meanwhile, however, the situation elsewhere had changed in his favour, and he was in a position to organize a fleet that should drive the Tyrians from the sea.

The Persian fleet in the Ægean was breaking up.

The kings, or, in the biblical term, judges, of Arvad and Byblos – they were really the magistrates of a commercial oligarchy – on news of their cities' surrender, broke away and went home. The Sidonian squadron followed their example; they had no love for Persia, and were bitterly jealous of Tyre. Then went the kings of Cyprus, both Phœnician and Greek. Alexander, summoning the returning squadrons to join him at Sidon – to which he took a strong force of troops to impress them – found himself with 223 galleys, including ten from Rhodes and exactly one from Macedonia.

While the fleet was mustering, Alexander went off in spring weather with his usual flying-column – 'the Hypaspistai, Agri-ânes and Archers' – over the Lebanon into the Beqaa valley, to teach a lesson to the hillmen, who had been attacking his supply columns. While there, characteristically, he risked his life by going back with a small party to bring in his old tutor and retainer, Lysimachos, who – true to the old 'Homer' game – had begged to be allowed to come, and had failed to go at light-infantry pace. Night fell on the group, sweat-drenched, cold and fireless; round about could be seen the fires of the Lebanese, who were dogging them at a respectful distance. Alexander went off over the rocks to one of the nearest fires, found two men sitting at it, killed them both with his dagger, and went back with a firebrand to his friends. The party kindled a large fire, success-fully beat off an attack made on them and rejoined the column next day.

Ten days after his departure he was back at Sidon, leaving all quiet in the Lebanon and Anti-Lebanon.

Work on the mole continued, the workers reinforced by thousands of skilled men from Cyprus and Phœnicia; but Alex-ander also mounted rams on horse-transports and on the older and slower battleships, with the project of attacking the less massive walls facing the sea.

The work was still very difficult. The Tyrians heightened their walls with wooden towers facing the mole, and shot incendiary arrows at the ships, making it dangerous to approach; and close enough approach to bring the rams into play proved physically impossible, as the shallows immediately below the walls were obstructed with massive rocks dumped there in the sea.

Alexander ordered these rocks to be hauled out with windlasses by galleys anchored offshore. The Tyrians sent out boats completely decked in – they must have looked like primitive submarines – to attack the anchor cables. Alexander equipped similar boats to defend them; but even then they were still cut under water by devoted Tyrian divers. The Macedonians substituted chains for ropes, and with immense labour the shallows were cleared.

By high summer the last stage of the siege was reached; but there was no sign of surrender. Rams mounted on the mole could make no impression on the landward wall, built of enormous stones set in cement. The Tyrians still fought with fanaticism, cutting themselves off from all hope of mercy by killing some Macedonian prisoners, captured earlier off Sidon, up on the wall, in full view of their friends. They now – King Azramelech and his ships having come home – attempted a sortie by sea, having screened their harbours some time before with sails to prevent observation of any preparations there. They did considerable damage to the Cypriote squadrons, catching them ashore during the siesta on a blazing summer afternoon; but Alexander in person, having returned, after a short rest, to the Sidonian ships on the other side of the island, caught them on their return and inflicted losses.

Rams mounted on ships now battered the seawalls, while archers gave covering fire. The south wall was breached, though a first assault by ships carrying drawbridges was beaten off.

Two days later, having waited for a dead calm, Alexander launched an all-out assault. Every archer and catapult-engine was in action. Naval squadrons threatened the harbours. At the south breach, battering-ships went in first, to disorganize the defence by bringing down some more of the wall. Then they retired, and the 'landing-craft' with their bridges in the bows came through, carrying the two storming parties, one of the Hypaspistai and one from Koinos' battalion.

The Hypaspistai went gallantly over the bridges and up the loose stones of the shattered wall; but for a time the Tyrians kept the advantage of their position. Admêtos, the leader of the first wave, fell on the summit of the breach. Then came the second wave of the assault, with Alexander. A footing was won; and then at once Macedonian armament and skill had an overwhelming advantage.

A minute later Koinos' battalion also gained its objective; and simultaneously the Cypriotes and Phœnicians stormed the two harbours. Alexander and the guards descended from the walls in a formed mass to break up the last organized resistance round the public buildings. For the rest it was massacre. Eight thousand Tyrians are said to have been killed, 30,000 – as at Thebes – sold to the slave dealers. Alexander spared only those who took sanctuary in the Temple of 'Hêrakles'; they included the King, and some ambassadors from Carthage. Afterwards he sacrificed there to his ancestor, and set up in the precincts the Tyrian Sacred Ship of Hêrakles and the ram which had first breached the wall, with an inscription so monstrous that Arrian judges it kindest not to give the words.

The siege had cost seven months' work and the lives of 400 Macedonians, in addition to allies; but it had finally removed the threat of a rising on Greece supported by Persian sea-power. Elsewhere, too, things were looking better. The Persian army from Armenia had reoccupied Cappadocia; but its repeated efforts to break through to the west had been brilliantly foiled by the Governor of Phrygia, Antigonos One-Eye, an old officer of Philip's. In arduous campaigns and with exiguous forces, Antigonos thrice repulsed the enemy in different parts of Asia Minor. Alexander's choice of a man, and his refusal to be diverted from Tyre, had been brilliantly justified.

During the siege also there arrived a second embassy from Dareios, this time with a 'firm' offer: 10,000 talents as ransom for his family, and the cession of all territory west of the

Euphrates. Alexander laid the matter before the Companions, according to custom; and from this meeting his most famous repartee is quoted. Parmenion said, 'I would accept that offer, if I were Alexander.' 'So would I,' said Alexander, 'if I were Parmenion.'

So Dareios continued his labours to raise another army; and Alexander, leaving Parmenion in Syria, marched on towards Egypt.

Even now the way to Egypt was not completely clear. Gaza, on its high 'tell' – the mound that already held the mud bricks and fallen tiles of over 2,000 years – was held for Dareios by a faithful officer named Batis. The siege of Tyre had given him ample time to collect supplies, strengthen the walls, and hire additional Arab troops; the Philistines – though by now they spoke Arabic or Phœnician – kept all their old stubbornness; and the height of the tell made it impossible for rams to reach the walls. So thought Batis; so said Alexander's engineers; whereat all Alexander's obstinacy rose up in arms. 'The more "impossible" it is, the more I will take it,' he said – *because of the moral effect*: or, in his own words, 'for the deed will dismay the enemy, and not to have taken it would disgrace me, when it was told to the Greeks and to Dareios.'

So – as at Tyre – the army was set to work to construct a vast ramp, up which the engines might reach the wall; but even when it was finished, the besieged fought on vigorously. Aristandros the Soothsayer, interpreting an omen, said one morning that Alexander would take the city, but must take care of his life today. Aristandros' prestige rose greatly as a result; for on that same day there was a sortie, and Alexander saw his engines on fire and his troops being driven backwards down the hill. Forgetting caution, he rushed with his guards into the fray; stopped the rout; but was struck down by a heavy bolt from an engine on the walls, which pierced him through shield and corselet into the shoulder. 'And he was healed with difficulty of that wound.'

Meanwhile the heavy siege-engines from Tyre were brought down by sea and set up; more ramps were thrown up; part of

the wall was battered down, other parts brought down by sap-
ping; and, covered by a storm of missiles which made it almost
certain death to stand on the walls, the Macedonians attacked
with ladders. Even then it was only at the fourth attempt that
sections of the wall were cleared, and then gate after gate was
reached and opened. This time few except women and children
survived to be sold as slaves. The Arabs and Philistines fought
on the walls and in the breaches and back to back in the streets
until practically every man was killed.

They had delayed Alexander for two months.

It is said that Alexander, having sustained a painful if not
serious blow on the leg from a stone in the last assault, while
his more serious wound was scarcely healed, showed no mercy
to Batis, who, having fought bravely, was brought before him
wounded, a repulsive figure, filthy with blood, dust and sweat,
but defiantly silent. Imitating the Achilles of the *Iliad* – and
if so, of an *Iliad* more savage than ours – he is said to have had
Batis' feet slit, straps passed through the wounds, and so to have
dragged him living behind his chariot till he died. This horrible story is told by the uncritical but not unlearned Roman
historian Quintus Curtius; it is not mentioned by Arrian, who
does tell, with regret, of other savage but less wanton cruel-
ties of Alexander. One can only hope that it is an invention of
Alexander's Greek enemies; but it is just as possible that it is
omitted by Arrian merely because it was suppressed by his
sources, Alexander's officers.

Afterwards he selected out of his spoils magnificent presents
for his mother and sister and other friends at home. To old
Leonidas he sent 500 talents' weight of frankincense and 100
of myrrh : the spices of Arabia which, as in the days of Solo-
mon, came up through Palestine to the Mediterranean ports.
He was having the last word over an incident in his boyhood
when he had wanted to throw a 'princely' double handful of the
costly stuff upon the altar-fire on a holy-day; and Leonidas had
stopped him saying, 'You must wait till you have conquered
the Spice-Country, my lad, before you lay it on like that.'

8   The Son of God

(Egypt, winter, 332–1)

Out of the clouds and rain of a second Syrian autumn
Alexander rode into the winter sunshine of Egypt. Mazakes, the
new Satrap, surrendered, having in any case no Persian troops
with which to hold his difficult province. Alexander rode at ease
in seven days across the Sinai Desert, and on via Heliopolis to
Memphis, the ancient equivalent of Cairo.

At Memphis he formally became Pharaoh of Egypt, as the
Persian kings had been, and did his best to conciliate the only
'educated class' of Egypt, the priests. To the flexible poly-
theism of Greece this was a relatively easy task, especially by
contrast with the hated Persians, monotheistic and doctrinaire.
Alexander sacrificed to Apis, whereas the Persian conqueror
Cambyses, it was said, had slaughtered the god's sacred bull.

He spent the winter organizing very carefully the administration of Egypt, whose economic importance and whose defensi-
bility, isolated behind its deserts and the difficult delta country,
had been long understood in Greece. The old general Iphikrates,
whose son was now with Alexander, had personally seen the
difficulties which the Persians had had in reconquering it against
no very formidable military force.

Alexander's system was an improved version of that of
Dareios the Great; its feature was an elaborate division of
functions, with different officers, civil, military and financial,
all reporting directly to the King.

Heads of the civil administration were two Egyptians, one
for Upper and one for Lower Egypt; though as one of them
shortly resigned and no satisfactory successor was to be found,
the two provinces were soon amalgamated. Two well-tried

Macedonian officers, Peukestas and Balakros, were left jointly in command of the troops in Egypt; but they were not in command of the Nile fleet, and even over the land forces their command seems to have been operational only. For routine matters, there were independent commanders for the two Macedonian garrisons (in Memphis at the head of the Delta and in the eastern frontier-fortress of Pelousion), and another officer again in command of the mercenaries; while for the latter there were also two inspectors, and a secretary who was one of Alexander's Companions presumably performing very much the functions of an adjutant-general. Finally there were separate Governors of Libya (Cyrenaica) and Sinai, the latter a local Greek, Kleomenes of Naukratis; Kleomenes was also to be treasurer for the whole of Egypt, with instructions to let the Egyptian Governors alone as long as they paid over the taxes to him punctually.

With all these officers responsible directly to him, Alexander felt that he had minimized as far as might be the danger that any person might try, like many nationalist leaders under Persia, to detach Egypt from the Empire.

But by no one was the significance of his precautions better understood than by that rising officer, Ptolemy, son of Lagôs.

It remained – since Egypt in Alexander's scheme of things was now to belong to the Mediterranean world – to provide the country with a worthy port, which should also be a Greek colony and a focus of Greek influence. There had been no such port hitherto, since neither Persian imperialism nor Egyptian nationalism had desired more contact than was found unavoidable; the old jealously regulated 'treaty-port' of Naukratis, on the western branch of the Nile, was quite inadequate. An open-sea port was required. The chief *desiderata* were:

(1) Proximity to the Delta, for the sake of inland water transport, while preferably avoiding the Delta itself, where shallow water and silt were to be expected.

(2) Sheltered deep-water anchorage.

(3) Fresh-water supply for a large town.

(4) Preferably, a western site on the shortest route to the Ægean.

A suitable site was found close to the western mouth of the Nile, between Lake Mareotis and the sea, where the shore is formed by an outcrop of rock, while a parallel outcrop, forming a long, narrow island (identified with Homer's mythical 'island of Pharos'), formed a natural break-water; and here Alexander founded the greatest of the many Alexandrias that were for a greater or less period to bear his name. A townplanner named Deinokrates was engaged, and Alexander himself 'marked the points in the city, where the shopping-centre was to be, and where the temples, and to what gods dedicated [including the gods of Greece and Isis of the Egyptians] and where the walled perimeter. And thereupon he sacrificed, and the omens were good.'

The whole transaction was marked by Alexander's usual clear-sighted efficiency. It was no startling stroke of genius, as is sometimes suggested; incidentally it may be remarked that Alexander founded many Alexandrias, and not all (or even most) of them had a long or distinguished career. Nor was Alexandria intended 'to replace Tyre'. It was hardly in a position to replace that great centre of trade with Armenia and Mesopotamia; moreover, that could be done by the other Phœnician cities and by resurgent Tyre itself.

While at Alexandria, also, 'the desire came upon him', says Arrian, 'to visit the shrine of Amon in Libya', at what is now, still sacred, the Oasis of Siva; 'both because the oracle of Amon was said to be unerring, and to have been consulted by Perseus and Hêrakles', whom 'Alexander had the desire to emulate, being descended from both of them; and because he was inclined to claim that Amon was his father, just as Zeus was the father of Hêrakles and Perseus'.

Amon (or 'Ammon') had long been identified with Zeus by the Greeks, to whom, moreover, the desert oracle, with its glamour of mystery, had long been known through the Greeks of Naukratis and Cyrene.

So Alexander went off with a small escort, not including, unfortunately, either of our two officer-historians, along the coast to Paraitonion (Matruh) and thence inland through the shifting sand-hills; a route not without perils for a caravan without the compass. Legend was busy very early with this march, even Ptolemy – who was not above glorifying with fable that which concerned his great predecessor's doings in Egypt – speaking of the caravan lost in the desert and guided to its goal by two serpents which spoke like men. Aristoboulos, on the other hand, speaks of signs of divine favour which do not sound supernatural; as, that the party were guided by birds flying towards the oasis, and that when they needed water, it rained heavily; which it emphatically can in the Western Desert, especially in winter.

There is therefore no reliable account of Alexander's dealings with the oracle; he appears himself to have said simply that he 'had heard what he wanted'; and he is reported, very credibly, to have asked if he had punished all the murderers of Philip. The answer was Yes. But for details we have only the stories collected by later writers, such as the charming but uncritical Plutarch.

A tradition, however, which goes back certainly to Alexander's own contemporaries, represents him as claiming in some fashion, from this time forth, to be the child of Zeus, and more specifically of Zeus-Ammon, the Greek adaptation of Amon of the Egyptians. Lysimachos the Body-Guard, when he became King of Thrace, was the first to put Alexander's head on his coins wearing the Ram's Horns of Amon, who had once been a ram-god. The type became classic, and Alexander in Eastern legend becomes Iskender *dhu'l-qarnein*, Alexander the Two-Horned.

The anti-Macedonian tradition in Greece, especially the school of Aristotle (which became very hostile to Alexander, for reasons which will appear), represents Alexander as developing from now on into a megalomaniac, who presently required men to bow before him as a god or put them to death if they refused. This is at least partly unfair to him. In his later attempt to enforce the 'kow-tow' – whose tragic history will be related – he was claiming reverence not as a god, but as King of Asia. Since in Greece one bowed before gods and not before men, it was easy, especially with a touch of malice, to misunderstand the matter.

The tendency of recent writers has therefore been to argue that Alexander merely became a God-King in Egypt in accordance with the custom of the country, just as he became an absolute (but not divine) King in Iran; and to make little of the alleged claim to divinity outside Egypt.

It is certainly true that Alexander continued in official documents to refer to Philip as his father; and there are stories, very credible, of Alexander, wounded, making jokes about 'ichor' (the 'blood' of the Gods, in Homer), or of Alexander amused, when it thundered, by the question of the philosopher-courtier Anaxarchos, 'Couldn't you do something like that, O son of Zeus?' Accordingly some recent writers conclude that Alexander took an entirely rationalist view of his alleged sonship of Zeus-Ammon, and merely used it, perhaps only in Egypt, as an instrument of statecraft.

This reaction probably goes too far.

It is important for our understanding of Alexander to remember his 'background'. The chief influence on his conscious mind in youth was Aristotle, whose philosophy, it is permissible to repeat, was teleological and religious. Behind Aristotle stood the stern Epirote Leonidas – no sceptical Athenian! and behind him in turn, the deepest influence of all, the influence of his unconscious mind, exerted in his earliest years, of Olympias.

Alexander, it is perfectly clear, was a 'churchgoer'. He did not go all the way to Siva merely to impress public opinion; he 'wanted to', for reasons given. He not only paid, but paid attention to a G.H.Q. Soothsayer; and he certainly, like most people in his age, believed implicitly in the historical reality of his 'ancestors' Achilles, Perseus, Hêrakles and the rest, even if (as with other historical characters) not all the stories about them were true.

But the old legends told that at least three of the gods –

Hêrakles, Dionysos and Asklêpios – as well as the 'Children of Zeus', the Dioskouroi – had been born on earth and had achieved divinity by 'heroic virtue' and power. Indeed, one school of philosophy suggested that *all* the Olympians had been heroic mortals.

It was surely natural that Alexander, brought up on the legends, descended from the heroes, conscious, without need of flattery, of dynamic powers far transcending those of ordinary men – even of his Macedonians; in youth regaled by his mother with dark hints that there had been something marvellous about his birth (Attalos may have been merely giving a nasty twist to these legends at the Bridal of Cleopatra) – that Alexander, conscious, if ever a man was, that he was a hero and a child of destiny, should, when hailed by Egyptian priests in their tremendous temples as the embodiment of the Living God, have pondered deeply in mind what manner of salutation this might be.

Egyptian religious thought did not deserve the prestige which it still had in Greece. Nevertheless, there were thoughtful Egyptians, and it is said to have been one such, named Psammon (perhaps he had in mind the Osiris ritual?), who explained to Alexander that every man is moved and ruled by a divine spirit; on which Alexander built his own recorded opinion, that while God was the common father of all, He made especially His own those who were best.

The King of Kings

(Egypt to Iran, 331–0)

Winter passed not unpleasantly for the troops in Egypt, enlivened, now that the Mediterranean was open, by musical and dramatic entertainments given by a troupe from Greece, including distinguished artists from Athens. In the Ægean, Pharnabazos, after being captured, had escaped; but Amphoteros, who had once more (finally) liberated Chios and Kos, was now free to deal with Crete and the Peloponnese.

Syria, meanwhile, had been restive, especially Palestine, where the Samaritans had killed their Macedonian Commissioner. Alexander, marching back that way in the spring, found it desirable to 'show the flag' extensively. He ended with a great durbar in Phœnicia, where the Athenian theatrical artists repeated their performances before Cypriote and Phœnician notables and Alexander's troops in Syria. As a result, one famous actor missed his engagement to play at the Dionysian dramatic festival in Athens, and was fined for it. He asked Alexander for a letter saying that he was absent by royal command; but Alexander refused thus to affront democratic feelings, and paid his fine for him instead.

Meanwhile Alexander dismissed his Governor of Syria for negligence and attended to other prosaic details. It was not until after mid-summer that the pontoon bridges, prepared in advance on the Euphrates, were swung out into position, and the army marched eastward, a small cavalry force under Mazaios, Satrap of Mesopotamia, retiring before them. Alexander's recruiting officers had been busy in Greece and Macedonia, despite all the enemy's attempts to create diversions; Kleandros had brought in 4,000 Peloponnesian mercenaries even at the most difficult time, before Tyre, and the army now numbered 7,000 cavalry and 40,000 foot.

Dareios, too, had called in his western army; the great satraps of the East had joined him, from the Caspian and the Oxus and the Hindu Kush; and effort had been made to improve equipment, by the issue, for example, of sabres to the light cavalry, hitherto armed only with javelins. An army greater by half than that of Issos now stood beyond the Tigris, in ideal 'cavalry country', with its back to the mountains of Media, where Dareios was personally known.

Dareios perhaps expected that Alexander would turn away, as before Issos, and make for Babylon. He could then be cut off – and without repeating the mistake of bringing the Persian army into a cramped position. But Alexander came on, skirting the foothills of the Armenian mountains, where water was still to be found after the rainless summer, and forded the Tigris, with difficulty though unopposed, in the foothills, where it flowed in wide, shallow rapids. Dareios made no attempt to defend the river line. He did not wish to fight in the hills; and he aimed, not at stopping Alexander, but at annihilation.

Soon after the crossing, a nearly total eclipse of the moon took place (the 20th September, 331 B.C.). Alexander, with a characteristic blend of science and religion, 'sacrificed to the Moon, and also to the Sun and Earth, because they are said to cause this phenomenon'. He then turned downstream. Three days after the crossing, the lancers made contact with enemy cavalry, and Ariston, the Paionian colonel, personally killed their leader, and, delighted with his exploit, brought the head back to Alexander. 'In my country,' he said, 'this gift would be rewarded with a gold cup.'

Alexander, who was at dinner, surveyed the bloody object without enthusiasm. 'Ah,' he said, 'but only an empty one. But I – see – will drink your health in a full one!' More important, however, the Paiones took prisoners, from whom it was learned that Dareios was close at hand, at the village of Gaugamêla.

Alexander halted again, fortified a camp in which to leave his heavy baggage, and gave his troops four days' rest. He then marched out about midnight to fall upon the enemy at dawn.

But when he sighted the enemy, at a distance of some four miles, on crossing a gentle rise in the ground, he saw something that gave him pause. The ground before him had been tampered with. Alexander at once suspected 'pottes' (to use Robert Bruce's expression) to catch his cavalry. He consulted the Companions. Most were for leading on; but Parmenion advised a further halt, and careful reconnaissance. Alexander agreed with him, and postponed the assault for twenty-four hours.

The ground proved not to have been undermined, but merely cleared and levelled; in fact, to facilitate the charge of war chariots, with which Dareios hoped to breach the deadly wall of spears of Alexander's phalanx. But the sight of the sheer size of the Persian army made many hearts beat faster, and even Parmenion proposed the desperate expedient of a night attack. Alexander rejected the proposal, saying he would not 'steal a victory'. It was not mere bravado, nor even merely the fact that a night battle would be a chancy affair. Alexander, as always, took the Napoleonic view of the importance of moral factors; he knew quite well that the Empire must be conquered, not by mere slaughter – for its man-power was practically inexhaustible – but by subduing the will of its fighting men, by the defeat of the best army which they could raise, on their own ground, in circumstances that left them no excuse or hope for better fortune another time.

Aristoboulos copied out a detailed account of Dareios' array from a captured document; but without detailed figures. Dareios had, Arrian tells us, 200 war chariots and about fifteen elephants. More had been ordered from India, but they were still on the road; Alexander captured them later at Susa. Those he had, effected nothing in the battle; probably they became unmanageable. He is further said to have had 40,000 cavalry, a figure which should probably be reduced by half (bodies of 1,000 and 2,000 cavalry are mentioned in a manner showing that they were no mere drop in the ocean).

For his infantry we have no reliable figures; but Alexander

realized that he was going to be outflanked on a formidable scale, and the elaborate care with which he drew up his line shows that he took the position very seriously indeed.

The nations of the north and north-west formed Dareios' right, under Mazaios, those of Persia proper and the farther east his left, under Bessos, Satrap of Bactria, warden of the north-eastern marches; of royal descent, and not unsuspected by Dareios of feeling that his claim to the throne was as good as Dareios' own. In his wing were his own Bactrian cavalry, both men and horses protected by scale-armour, and hordes of savage nomads from central Asia, whom the Greeks vaguely called Scythians, with flat brutish faces and matted hair.

Next to them were the Persians and neighbouring Iranian nations, horse and foot, forming the left-centre; while the nomad horse-archers and 1,000 Bactrians were thrown forward in advance of the left wing. Mazaios on the right had, similarly thrown forward, his heavy cavalry from Armenia and Cappadocia, the cradle, in a later age, of the armoured knight. After them came Arab horsemen from the Syrian desert; then his Medes and other Iranian horse and foot, and nearest the centre, probably his best infantry, Caucasian mountaineers.

In the centre, after the fiasco at Issos, there were no Kardakes this time; there were simply the best available men, with their accustomed weapons: Nabarzanes' own Persian Guard, the 10,000 'Immortals'; the Greeks, probably only those 4,000 now, who had followed Dareios from Issos; Karians from the Ægean, who had been so inconveniently warlike in their own country that they had been deported inland; mountaineers from Afghanistan, Persian horse-guards and some Indian cavalry, and the Mardian archers from the Elburz range. These were posted on the left centre, facing Alexander. Behind these, hordes of peasant infantry from Babylonia, of little military value, served to deepen the mass.

Dareios, as usual, was in the centre on his 'command vehicle', his faithful Greeks massed around him, and in front his fifteen elephants with their Indian drivers. In front of the whole line were the chariots, in four groups of fifty; one group on the right, one, with the elephants, in the centre, and two in front of the left and left-centre, where Alexander might be expected; formidable battle-wagons, which had once at least broken Greek pikemen in Asia Minor; much heavier than those which caused such consternation among Cæsar's legions in Britain, and with scythe-blades projecting from their axles and shafts.

Alexander was confident that he could win if he could deliver one knockout blow with his heavy cavalry and phalanx at the enemy's nerve centre, Dareios himself. There could be no question of defeating such a horde (*en venir à bout*, as the French say) by mere slaughter. But in the Persian Empire men fought for the King. Dareios himself must be killed, taken or driven from the field; and Alexander, who had seen him at Issos, knew that Dareios was a man who gave up too soon.

To prevent just such a blow the enemy would make every effort to bring his line to a standstill by attacking its flanks, forcing units to face outward for defence. If they succeeded, the position would be serious. Simultaneously, the chariots and elephants would try to disorder his front.

In face of these threats, Alexander drew up his army in depth. His formation was not merely, as is sometimes said, 'a hollow square'; it was neither so geometric nor so primarily defensive. Rather his plan was to draw up his heavy shock troops in their accustomed order – Horse-Guards, Hypaspistai, Phalanx, Erigyios' Greek cavalry, Thessalians – covered in front and rear, and especially on the flanks, by other units, whose duty was to prevent the enemy from interfering with their advance.

Parmenion would accompany the Thessalians on the left, commanding in chief all troops to the left of Krateros' brigade (inclusive).

At each end of his line were defensive wings or flank guards, their units lying back in échelon; on the right, half the Agriânes, half the Macedonian archers, and a veteran Greek infantry regiment, the 'Old Mercenaries', under Kleandros, son of Polemokrates; on the left, Cretan archers, Thracian javelin-men under

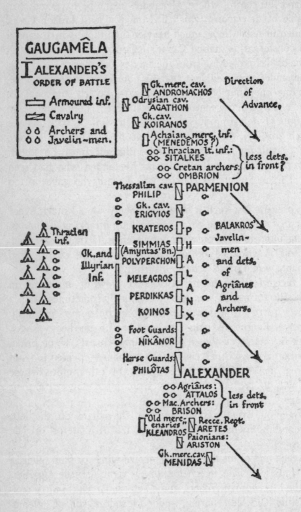

GAUGAMÊLA

ALEXANDER'S ORDER OF BATTLE

▭ Armoured inf.
▱ Cavalry
∘∘ Archers and
∘∘ Javelin-men.

Gk. merc. cav.
ANDROMACHOS

Odrysian cav.
AGATHON

Gk. cav.
KOIRANOS

Achaian merc. inf.
(MENEDEMOS?)

Thracian lt. inf.:
SITALKES

Cretan archers:
OMBRION

} less dets. in front?

Direction of Advance.

Thessalian cav.
PHILIP

Gk. cav.
ERIGYIOS

PARMENION

KRATEROS

SIMMIAS
(Amyntas' Bn.)

POLYPERCHON

MELEAGROS

PERDIKKAS

KOINOS

P H A L A N X

Thracian inf.

Gk. and Illyrian Inf.

BALAKROS
Javelin-men and dets. of Agriânes and Archers.

Foot Guards:
NÎKÂNOR

Horse Guards:
PHILÔTAS

ALEXANDER

Agriânes:
ATTALOS

Mac. Archers:
BRISON

} less dets. in front

"Old merc-
enaries"
KLEANDROS

Recce. Regt.
ARETES

Paionians:
ARISTON

Gk. merc. cav.
MENIDAS.

their native officer Sitalkes, Greek mercenaries from Achaia. In front of the right wing were Aretes' and Ariston's lancers, and Menidas' Greek mercenary cavalry; and similarly outside the left wing, but apparently lying *back* (for the left was to be the refused or defensive wing), two more regiments of Greek and one of Thracian cavalry. The remaining archers and javelin-men covered the front of the main line, with the mission especially of dealing with chariots.

Lastly the Illyrian and remaining Greek infantry formed a second line in rear of the centre to guard it against attacks from the rear. Camp and baggage were left under guard of the Thracian infantry.

Having made these dispositions, Alexander bade the troops take their supper, and summoned all officers. He outlined his plan, emphasized the supreme nature of the test, and bade them pass on his words to their men, demanding especially strict discipline, care over the prompt and accurate passing of orders, silence in the ranks, and then that every man should shout the 'Alalai!' with the full strength of his lungs when the time came.

The army lay down to sleep in its battle positions. Alexander sent for Aristandros the prophet and sacrificed to the gods, and especially to the demon Terror (whose personal existence was attested in the *Iliad*), that he would stretch out his hand over the enemy's army. Then, his work done, he went to his tent, and fell almost at once into a deep slumber.

Four miles away a glow of fire moved up and down. The Great King was inspecting his troops under a blaze of torch-light. The Persian army stood to arms all night, in fear of attack, and it was a weary host that saw the plains turn grey in the false dawn, with a white ground-mist filling the shallow depression between the lines.

Alexander slept on till the sun was high in the sky. The troops were up and had breakfasted and were waiting for orders. At last Parmenion ventured to wake him, marvelling that he could sleep so soundly.

'Why not?' said Alexander gaily. 'The time for worrying was *before* we had brought the enemy to battle.'

Even now he was in no hurry. He put on his corselet – not of metal, but of two thicknesses of linen cord – mounted a palfrey (he kept the now ageing Boukephalas for the charge) and rode, Aristandros beside him in white robes and priestly circlet of gold, to encourage the Greeks on his left, who would not have his personal leadership in the battle. Kallisthenes' official history told how, standing before the Thessalians, he raised his right hand to heaven and prayed aloud to the gods : 'If I am indeed the son of Zeus, now defend and strengthen the Hellenes!'

Then he rode back, took his position at the head of the Companions with Philôtas, Kleitos, and Hêphaistion, and signalled for the whole army to advance, obliquely to the right, towards the enemy's flank. The Persians tried to conform to this movement, which must have been difficult with their less well-trained troops.

As the distance lessened, the nomad horse-archers, riding parallel, began to shoot into Alexander's covering troops. The Macedonians were beginning to get clear of the ground which had been levelled for the chariots, when Dareios ordered his left wing to ride round their flank and stop this sidelong move. The 'Scythians' and the thousand mailed Bactrians in advance of Bessos' line trotted threateningly forward, and Alexander in turn ordered Menidas to stop their movement.

Menidas and his men went bravely in, but they were too few; Alexander almost at once had to send the Paionian lancers and Kleandros' mercenaries in support. Before their charge the enemy gave way; but then came up the main body of the Bactrians, and a severe fight ensued, 'Alexander's men losing more heavily than the enemy, being so greatly outnumbered, and because the Scythians, both horses and men, had better defensive armour; yet even so, they met the enemy's attacks and, charging violently by squadrons, even gained ground.' Menidas himself fell wounded, but his men were doing well enough. Alexander let them struggle and kept his remaining lancer regiment in hand.

'Meanwhile,' continues Arrian, 'the barbarians loosed their

scythed chariots against Alexander himself; and this was their greatest disappointment ...'

These great vehicles were, in fact, fearfully vulnerable to *steady* light troops. Most skirmishers of that day were not steady; but Alexander's were. They waited coolly, dodged, and slammed in their javelins. Chariot after chariot crashed with a horse down, or swerved and lost way, while the Agriânes and Balakros' javelin-men, not without loss themselves, grabbed at the traces and tore down the charioteers. Only a few reached the main battle-line, where the Macedonians, with parade-ground precision, opened their ranks and let them through. The horses, swerving from the spear-points, tore harmlessly down the lanes opened, and were rounded up in rear.

But behind the chariots Dareios' whole line was now advancing, while Mazaios' cavalry swung round after Parmenion's flank as it moved away from them. Three thousand of them rode straight past that flank and overran Alexander's camp, overwhelming the Thracians and massacring the unarmed cooks, drivers and servants, while the prisoners broke loose and joined in the mêlée.

The two infantry lines were now only a few hundred yards apart. Bessos' cloud of cavalry, turning Alexander's right, was still extending and growing heavier; though, worried by the vicious, controlled, small-scale charges of the gallant mercenaries and lancers, they had still not reached the flank of the main line. But it appears that, in the Persian leftward movement, Bessos' cavalry had moved farther and faster than the infantry centre, as one would expect, with troops whose drill did not reach Macedonian standards. And now, as more and more cavalry reinforced the wing that was fighting, a gap opened at the 'hinge' between them and Dareios' infantry centre. It was the opportunity of a lifetime; Alexander may well have anticipated it. He sent his last flank-guards, Aretes' lancers and the Agriânes, against Bessos, and prepared to charge the gap.

And then a message arrived from Parmenion saying that he was heavily engaged, his flank turned, the baggage lost and he needed help.

Alexander considered this untimely.

'Tell Parmenion,' he said, 'that if we win we shall have the enemy's baggage; and if we do not, every brave man will be dead.'

If the Thessalians could not join in the assault, it must take place without them. Alexander put on his helmet and gave the order to change direction left and charge. He himself with the horse-guards rode headlong for Dareios' exposed flank; and foot-guards and phalanx with levelled spears and yelling their 'Alalai!' bore down at the *pas de charge* upon his centre.

The charge was not 'as if on parade'. The lighter-armed foot-guards were ahead of the phalanx, and the two left battalions of the phalanx hung back, keeping in touch with Parmenion, who had now been brought to a standstill. Not a level line, but aslant, 'like the ram of a ship', as Arrian says, rolled across the last 200 yards, while the Mardian archers poured in their shafts at them. Koinos and Perdikkas fell wounded by arrows at the head of their phalanx battalions; but still the line of sarissas came on unbroken, crashed irresistibly into archers, mercenaries and Persian Guards, and dug its way murderously towards the high chariot of the King. For a few minutes there was furious hand-to-hand fighting; but the long pikes were too much for any courage with inferior weapons. With Alexander and the Companions driving in from the flank, the front crumbled rapidly. Soon, while the slaughter of his guards came closer and closer to his chariot, which could not be turned in the press, Dareios alighted from it, and, finding panic growing round him, just as at Issos, mounted a swift mare and made off to the rear.

The centre dissolved round him. Almost simultaneously Bessos' cavalry, seeing the centre broken, gave way before the charge of Aretes' lancers.

The victory had been won, and quickly, but yet with no time to spare. Mazaios was still pressing Parmenion hard; and there had nearly been a serious disaster in the centre. Parmenion and the left of the phalanx being halted, a gap had opened between the fourth and fifth battalions, and a torrent of Persian

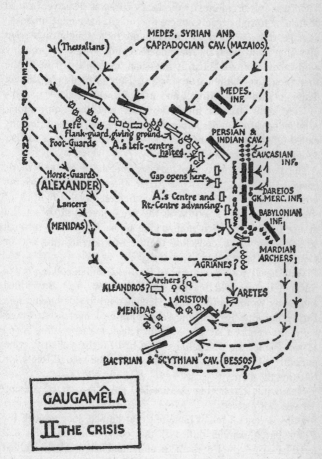

MEDES, SYRIAN AND
CAPPADOCIAN CAV. (MAZAIOS).

(Thessalians)

LINES OF ADVANCE

MEDES.
INF.

Left
Flank-guard, giving ground.
Foot-Guards

A.'s Left-centre
halted.

PERSIAN &
INDIAN CAV.

CAUCASIAN
INF.

Gap opens here.

Horse-Guards
(ALEXANDER)

DAREIOS
GK. MERC. INF.

A.'s Centre and
Rt.-Centre advancing.

Lancers

BABYLONIAN
INF.

(MENIDAS)

MARDIAN
ARCHERS

AGRIANES ?

KLEANDROS ?   Archers ?

ARETES

MENIDAS   ARISTON

BACTRIAN & "SCYTHIAN" CAV. (BESSOS)
?

GAUGAMÊLA

II THE CRISIS

horse-guards and Indian cavalry poured through it, inside Alexander's 'square'.

Once more discipline, or the lack of it, was decisive. Instead of turning to right or left, where they might have done immense damage, this roaring tide of men simply rode straight on. Arrian says that *they* overran Alexander's camp, which is probably a mistake; they would hardly have had time. In any case, by the time they turned, the battle was lost. They formed up again in a dense column of squadrons, and started to ride back.

They rode straight into Alexander and the Companions, Alexander, after a desperate effort to reach Dareios, having called off the pursuit and turned back in response to a further agonized appeal from Parmenion.

The two great masses of cavalry met head on, and there, irrelevantly, took place what Arrian (probably from Ptolemy, who will have been in it) calls the 'fiercest cavalry fighting of the whole action ... not with the usual javelin-throwing and manoeuvring, but each man trying to hack his way through straight before him, conscious that he was now fighting not for victory but for dear life.'

With heavy loss, a remnant of the Indo-Iranian column broke through and escaped, leaving the Companions, less sixty killed and many wounded (including Hêphaistion) to ride on and join Parmenion. But by this time Parmenion no longer needed their help; the report that the King had fled was spreading along Mazaios' line; the Thessalians, who had fought gallantly, were pursuing a beaten foe, and infantry from the second line were retaking the camp.

Meanwhile the fleeing Dareios had got a long start. Alexander was not pleased.

Many a general might have felt that he had done enough for a day; but Alexander rallied all that could still ride of his battered cavalry – the Companions alone had had 500 horses killed – and was away in pursuit, leaving Parmenion to secure elephants, camels, treasure and hordes of prisoners in Dareios' camp at Gaugamêla.

Alexander rode until dusk; bivouacked for a few hours at

the River Lykos; started again at midnight (moonrise – it was seven days after the eclipse), and by next evening rode into Dareios' base at Arbêla, sixty miles from the field. Here he captured more vast quantities of stores; but it was impossible to pursue farther. Dareios, rejoined by the Bactrian cavalry, 2,000 Greeks and a remnant of the Immortals, and abandoning all hope of defending Babylon or Susa, had fled through the mountains into Media.

The bridge over the Lykos was intact. Dareios' party had proposed to demolish it after passing, but Dareios – it is characteristic of the man – had said No; better that the enemy should have the use of it than that still more of his own men should perish to no purpose.

Alexander rode into Babylon, Mazaios, as Satrap, surrendering the city and province. He was the first of the greater Iranian nobles to give in, probably feeling that he had done his duty at Gaugamêla and that if Dareios deserted his servants who were still fighting, his servants need do no more for him. If the war, as Alexander said, was about who was to be King of Kings, there was no doubt who was the better man.

Mazaios had already sent his son to meet Alexander, and may not have been surprised when Alexander requested him to remain civil Governor of his enormous Satrapy. As in Egypt, Alexander appointed a Macedonian (a Greek of Amphipolis) as 'G.O.C. troops', and another Greek, also reporting independently, as finance officer. Simultaneously he appointed the Persian who had surrendered Sardis as Governor of Armenia. He could spare few European troops to police these great provinces, and he gave their commanders discretion to recruit natives into the Macedonian army. The whole group of measures constituted a new policy, which he was to apply generally east of the Euphrates.

He also, as in Egypt, conciliated the priests and the Chaldean 'wise men', and with ancient ceremonial 'took the hands of Bel' as King of Babylon; a title which had been borne by the early Persian kings, but abandoned by Xerxes after the Babylonian revolt. Xerxes had also on that occasion sacked the great Temple of Bel, giving to Alexander the welcome opportunity of decreeing its restoration.

Funds were not lacking, for news came in that Susa, the chief imperial capital – 'Shushan the Palace' of the Jewish scriptures – had surrendered to a column under the Companion Philoxenos, and the bullion captured there amounted to 50,000 talents of gold – 4,200,000,000 drachmas. The spoils of ancient wars of conquest were there, too, including spoils of Athens taken by Xerxes. Among these were the statues, queer and archaic to the eyes of Alexander's men, of the tyrant-slayers Harmodios and Aristogeiton, set up about 500 B.C. by the young democracy. Alexander restored them to Athens, where for 600 years they stood side by side with the group that had replaced them in 477; a self-contained illustration of the rise of classical sculpture.

Alexander stayed in Babylon for six weeks. The troops enjoyed themselves and Dareios heard (no doubt a calculated leak) that they were demoralized by wine and women. It lulled his suspicions. Alexander was really planning a tremendous piece of exploitation of his victory.

Early in December he marched for Susa, some 400 miles in twenty days, and thence sent 3,000 talents under escort to Antipatros for the war with Sparta. King Agis had failed to do anything effective in Alexander's most difficult hour. The time had now come to make an end of him.

At Susa also he settled in comfort Dareios' mother and daughters; his wife had died in Syria. For the province of Susiana he made arrangements similar to those for Babylonia. Then, though winter was falling, he took the mountain road that led to the heart of Persia and her oldest capitals at Persepolis and Pasargadai.

On the way he received a message from the chiefs of the mountain Ouxians. The Ouxians of the plain were a peaceable people, who had fought, or been present, at Gaugamêla without leaving any mark in history. Their mountain cousins, on the other hand, in their eyries in the heart of the Persian Empire, had never, they said, paid tribute to any Persian king; and they would now be glad to receive from the new King the blackmail which they had been accustomed to have from Dareios and his predecessors for unmolested passage through their hills.

Alexander must have laughed inwardly as he replied that if the Ouxians would kindly meet him in the pass, they should have 'what was coming to them'.

Then, with some 10,000 men and guides from Susiana – probably by no means unwilling – he took a mountain path by night, fell at dawn upon the mountain valley of the hillmen, and thence, leaving a trail of fire and blood, came down to the highway in rear of the assembled warriors. They, in dismay, broke away to the hills – and were ambushed by Krateros, whom Alexander had detached to hold the line by which he thought the quarry would be most likely to break.

The Ouxians had 'had it'. All resistance was at an end, and Alexander was able without anxiety – after entreaties, including those of the kind-hearted Queen-Mother Sisygambis – to let them stay in their mountains, paying a heavy tribute in sheep, as they had no money.

There was more serious opposition ahead. The Persian homeland still held the remnant of a line that had marched with the great Cyrus, and would not fall without a struggle. The Satrap Ariobarzanes, with 700 horse and a few thousand infantry, walled up the pass that led into Persia, and held it; a Persian Thermopylæ, and like Thermopylæ it fell. Guided by prisoners and leaving a third of his force in camp under Krateros, Alexander again took to the hills by night, 'by a difficult path and a rough one, yet he took most of it at full speed'. One presumes there was a moon. Nevertheless, there was a nightmare episode at one point, where the path had been carried away by a landslip, and they had to struggle through a thick wood ... While it was still dark they rushed Ariobarzanes' mountain outposts, and at first light they were on the road behind the wall, while the trumpets signalled to Krateros to advance. Meanwhile parties under Amyntas, Philôtas and Ptolemy were already bridging a river on the road to Persepolis farther ahead.

Only Ariobarzanes with a handful of horsemen escaped to the open flank, over the forested hills. Alexander swept on, and again arrived in time to secure the treasury before its guards could loot it. Approaching Persepolis also, the army met with a pathetic welcome from a crowd of political prisoners, released or broken loose from the state dungeons; filthy, verminous, half-starved, many of them mutilated, in accordance with the barbarous Persian custom. There were many Greeks among them.

Then there was a longer rest for the troops, many of whom had marched 1,500 miles since the spring, apart from operations. There was winter merrymaking in the palaces of the kings of Persia, during which the 'old knight' Dêmarâtos of Corinth burst into tears for joy to see Alexander seated on the throne of Cyrus, and a Persian butler for grief to see Dareios' inlaid supper-table thrust under Alexander's feet as a footstool by a Macedonian page. Alexander also burnt down the palace of Xerxes at Persepolis 'in revenge for Athens'. Arrian does not mention, and modern writers, perhaps unnecessarily, dismiss as fantasy the story that he was prompted to do it, at a banquet, by an Athenian girl, the courtesan Thaïs, mistress of Ptolemy; but it is a fact at least that this harking back to the 'war of revenge' comes as an aberration at this time, when he was already developing his new policy, conciliating the Persians, over whom he was to rule.

During this winter, Alexander subdivided his cavalry squadrons into 'companies' (the infantry word); raised a new regiment of mounted javelin-men, probably Asiatic; and arranged for the training of 30,000 young Persians as Macedonian soldiers. The whole manpower of Persia proper was thus denied to the enemy.

He also saw a good deal of the captive Queen-Mother and of Dareios' daughters, one of whom, Stateira, he was – long after, and for reasons of state – to marry. No doubt he found again in the old Queen something that reminded him of his mother. As 'Mother' he addressed her, as he had addressed Queen Ada in

Karia, and like a Persian son he used to stand in her presence till she invited him to sit down. A charming story, that rings true, is also told of how he made Sisygambis a present of some Macedonian clothing which had just been sent out to him, and suggested innocently that her granddaughters might pass the time by learning to make such things themselves. There was consternation in the forlorn little court, and Alexander found that no great Persian lady ever demeaned herself by making clothes, and that the princesses thought they were being made slaves. Alexander laughed, and told them that the tunic which he himself was wearing had been made by his sisters.

In such fashion Alexander perfected his appreciation of the difference that lay between Persian monarchy and that of the simple 'Homeric' world at home.

Four hundred miles to the north-west, at the old summer capital of Ecbatana in Media (Hamadan), Dareios spent the winter in anguish of soul; still the Great King, still with every luxury and approached with deep prostrations; but shaken by the rout of his army, the loss of his capitals, the defection of Mazaios; suspicious – with reason – even of Bessos and Nabarzanes, who remained with him; his wife dead in captivity, his mother and daughters still prisoners, and treated with a kindness for which his tortured mind could imagine no creditable reason.

Bessos and Nabarzanes were still anxious to make a fight for Iran, but agreed, since Gaugamêla, that Dareios was not the man to lead it. Nabarzanes and Barsaëntes, Satrap of Arachosia (Afghanistan), were prepared to support Bessos as King. To dethrone Dareios would present no difficulties, since they controlled practically all the troops present, except the remaining Greeks. On the other hand, it might be best not to upset Iran still further by another revolution, if they wished to call out the eastern contingents again for a campaign in the spring.

Across this question cut the purely military one. Should Media be defended in another pitched battle? Could the army, which could be raised, at least defend mountain passes? Dareios, in desperation, was for fighting, and according to Alexander's intelligence had called out the still powerful contingents from the north-eastern frontier provinces. Bessos, on the other hand, was for retreating on Bactria – his own country, where it would be all the easier to realize his secret project – 'scorching the earth' as they went, and letting the deserts, the vast distances and Macedonian war-weariness fight for them.

In the circumstances it is not surprising that, in fact, no army had materialized, when, with the first swallows, came the news that Alexander had left Persepolis, on the march against them.

Alexander's object was now to seize the person of Dareios, preferably alive. He probably intended – with the personal ascendancy which he could easily gain – to secure from him a formal abdication in the conqueror's favour. Afterwards, his mild character would have fitted him excellently to rule a province, as conquered kings had often done under Persia; perhaps even as King of Persia, suitably watched by Macedonian officers, under Alexander as the Great King, King of the Kings of Asia.

Three days short of Ecbatana, he learned from a deserter – a surviving son of Ochos, the late King – that Dareios was retreating, five days ahead, with some 9,000 men, of whom 3,000 were cavalry, and the treasure from Ecbatana, about 7,000 talents.

At Ecbatana he halted briefly. War-weariness was general in his army, and with the occupation of the last of the great capitals he decided to dispense with the Greek Allied contingents, the part of his forces over which he had the least disciplinary control. He paid off the Thessalians and the Greek League troops and arranged for their journey home. Any who wished, he added, might enrol individually for paid service in his army; and many did so. He was working towards an imperial 'new model' army, unified, and completely under the control of the King.

He ordered Parmenion, with the bulk of the Greeks and Thracians, to bring up the treasure from Persia and Susa to Ecbatana (which was more central), where Harpalos would be in charge of it, and thereafter to secure the country northward to the Caspian. Then, with his best troops – the Macedonians, archers, Agriânes, lancers and Erigyios' Greek cavalry – he marched out after Dareios, now reported, with a long wagon-train, on the road to Rhagai, south of the Caspian, 400 miles away.

The speed of this march was terrific; 'men fell out and horses foundered,' says Arrian, 'but he led on and reached Rhagai on the eleventh day'. But Dareios, his army dwindling from desertions, had already fled, through the mountain pass of the Caspian Gates. Alexander rested his army for five days. Then he advanced in two days, through the pass, and sent Koinos out to forage, because he heard that the country ahead was desert.

Meanwhile two deserters came in : a son of Mazaios and a leading Babylonian named Bagistânes. They brought the news that Dareios had been put under arrest by Bessos, Nabarzanes and Barsaëntes. 'Hearing this,' continues Arrian, 'Alexander pushed on yet more urgently, with only the Companions and the Lancers and a few picked light infantry, without even waiting for Koinos to come in ... They carried nothing but their arms and food for two days. He marched all night and till noon on the following day; rested for a short time, marched again all night, and came at dawn to the camp from which Bagistânes had turned back; but the enemy were not there. Here he learned that Dareios was being carried away prisoner in a carriage, while Bessos had been acknowledged as leader by the Bactrian cavalry and the rest of the barbarians, except Artabazos and his sons. The Greek mercenaries were also faithful to Dareios, but were helpless to prevent what was being done.'

These Greeks were, with the personal loyalty of their race, the last faithful soldiers of the unhappy Dareios. A few days earlier, their commander, one Patron, obtaining audience with difficulty and speaking in Greek (which Dareios understood, but Bessos, who was present, did not), had warned him that there was a plot hatching among the Bactrians. His own men, he said, were loyal, and he begged Dareios to make them his sole bodyguard. They would see that he came to no harm.

Dareios thanked his servant, but refused. The report only

confirmed his own suspicions; but if his only chance was to trust himself to foreigners against his own Persians, he felt he might as well make an end.

Patron then led his men off the road and, in Greek fashion, took to the hills. Dareios' only supporters now were the westernized family of Artabazos. His arrest followed shortly.

'When Alexander heard of this, he deemed it time to pursue at full speed. Men and horses were dropping with fatigue, but he still led on. They made a long march that night and up till noon the next day, and came to a village where Dareios and his captors had halted the day before. Then, hearing that the Persians had determined to march by night, he questioned the villagers as to whether they knew of a shorter way. They said they did, but it was all desert; there was no water. He told them to show him that way; and realizing that the infantry would not be able to keep up, he dismounted 500 cavalry, chose out the file-leaders and the strongest other infantry, and bade them ride, with their infantry weapons. He sent Nîkânor, the commander of the Hypaspistai, and Attalos, commander of the Agriânes, by the road which Bessos had followed ... Then, starting at nightfall, he went fast. They covered fifty miles that night and, about dawn, overtook the barbarians, travelling in disorder and unready. Few of them showed fight; most, as soon as they saw Alexander himself, fled without striking a blow; and those who fought fled also before many had been killed.

'Bessos and his companions went on for a while, dragging Dareios in his carriage; but when Alexander was close upon them, Nabarzanes and Barsaëntes stabbed Dareios and left him; and they fled with six hundred horsemen.'

Alexander and his last sixty stalwarts rode on from the scene of the skirmish. They rode over silver and gold that had been thrown away, and past wagon-loads of women and children wandering driverless; pushing on after the foremost, where they supposed Dareios would be. At last someone looked into a carriage whose mules had turned aside into a pool of water and were drinking. In it was Dareios, bleeding to death. He asked for water, which was given him; thanked the giver,

and bade him thank Alexander for his kindness to his mother
and wife and children. Soon afterwards he died. Alexander, who
had ridden on, came back, too late to speak with him. He
covered the body with his cloak and directed that it should be
sent to Persia to lie in the tombs of the kings.

10 The Increasing Strain

(Iran, 330–327)

With the capture of Ecbatana and death of Dareios, the character of the war changed. No more great battles were to be expected, at least in Iran; it remained only to consolidate. This meant dealing with the north-eastern barons who remained in arms; subduing the mountain regions which the Persians had left alone; and then an expedition to conquer India, imagined as a region of no overwhelming extent, bounded, a few marches beyond the Indus, by the outer sea. Alexander was already beyond the limits of the world known to Greek geographers; those with him counted the Hindu Kush as part of the Caucasus, and believed the Syr Darya to be the upper reaches of the Don. After thus 'clearing up' Asia, he planned to return home and round off his conquests northward by a largely sea-borne expedition to the Black Sea coasts.

The army reunited at Zadrakarta, south-east of the Caspian. Somewhere hereabout a gang of horse-thieves carried out one of the greater achievements of their profession by stealing Boukephalas, whereat Alexander, in a fury, threatened, if the horse was not brought back, to depopulate the whole district. The horse was brought back.

Meanwhile many of the chiefs who had remained with Dareios came in and surrendered: old Artabazos, whom Alexander honoured for his loyalty to his late King, with his three sons; Phrataphernes, Satrap of Parthia, where the army now was, and Satibarzanes of Areia to the south-east; Alexander confirmed them in their satrapies. Nabarzanes, perhaps doubtful of his reception, sent a letter offering submission; Alexander thought it expedient to accept it; Nabarzanes surrendered and passes from history. Emissaries also came, asking for terms, from the last 1,500 of Dareios' Greek mercenaries 'somewhere in the mountains', where they had evaded a column under Krateros. Alexander, as usual, demanded unconditional surrender, adding that the mercenaries had done great wrong in fighting for Persia against the League of united Greece; but as he sent this reply by the hands of Artabazos, whom they knew well, and of Andronîkos, an officer who sympathized with them, hints may have been dropped that they need not be afraid. Not long afterwards they came in, and with them Greek Ambassadors sent before the war to Dareios from Athens, Sparta, Sinôpe on the Black Sea and Chalkêdon on the Bosphorus. Alexander kept the Athenians and Spartans as prisoners; set free those from the cities in Asia, and the soldiers who had served Dareios since before the formation of the League; and formally condemned the others – but only to the 'penalty' of serving him, at their old rate of pay, as a new regiment under Andronîkos.

While waiting for them, he carried out a fierce and bloody raid into the mountains to subdue the brave and independent Mardians.

Greece was at last no longer dangerous. News had come in that Antipatros, though delayed by a serious situation in Thrace, where the Getai had defeated and killed the military governor Zôpyrion, had at last been able to deal with Sparta. While he was in Thrace, King Agis had united or coerced most of the Peloponnese; but the great centre of Megalopolis held out against him; Antipatros came down, reinforced by the cities that held to the League; and Agis fell, with a quarter of his army, after a desperate struggle with 22,000 men against 40,000.

Greece seemed very small and far away to Alexander now. He passed Antipatros' dispatch to Hêphaistion, saying, with a quotation from a famous parody, 'It seems that while we have been conquering the East, there has been some Battle of the Frogs and Mice in Arcadia.'

He was still Captain of the League, though he had sent home its contingents 'on completion of mission', and he acted as such in dealing with Dareios' mercenaries; still King of Macedonia, and as such socially only first among his peers; but his new character as King of Asia, especially since he was *in* Asia, tended to eclipse the other two. As such he had to deal with Persians. There simply were not enough Macedonians and Greeks to govern the whole empire, even if he had tried. He had learned to respect Persians for their gallantry in battle, and even for their efficiency, up to a point, though Persian administration had an Oriental capacity for letting things slide if they were not immediately necessary. He was now beginning to find Persian company congenial for another reason.

He was not yet twenty-six. In six years he had won greater victories than any hero in Greek history had won in a lifetime, and he had done it, at several turning-points, in the teeth of all advice from his generals and Companions. Yet to them, however much they genuinely admired him, he was still only first among his peers, the man they had known as a boy, addressed, Greek fashion, by his name, or at most as 'King', *tout court*. Moreover the Companions were proud of themselves, as well as of Alexander, and Alexander's lavish distributions of plunder, such as no conqueror before him had ever seen, seemed to have the effect, in their eyes, of increasing not so much his stature as their own. The continued austerity of Alexander's own life, and the simplicity of his diet, produced no effect on the habits of vulgar luxury and ostentation into which they readily dropped. Philôtas, during the winter in Persia, is said to have gone hunting with twelve miles of nets into which to drive the game. Leonnâtos had soft sand for his gymnasium sent to him by special camel-train from Egypt. Hagnon, an Ionian captain, had silver nails in his boots. The son of Mazaios said to Alexander, when declining the offer of a larger satrapy in addition to one which he had : 'Sire, in the old days there was one Dareios; but now you have made many Alexanders!'

Alexander would have been scarcely human if he had not found something congenial, something which he felt was his due, in the courtly obsequiousness with which men like Mazaios and Artabazos approached and addressed their King.

It was in part, no doubt, to win the confidence of his new subjects that, during this summer, he began to wear the comfortable and civilized Iranian native dress of embroidered jacket and trousers, though not in its most elaborate Median form, and not, at first, on any public occasions.

The Macedonians felt that their King was moving away from them, and resented it. They feared more than they need have; no Persian, in fact, ever became Alexander's personal friend on the footing on which many Macedonians were; but the anxiety was there. Even Kallisthenes once begged him, 'Do not forget Greece because we are few and in a strange land.' For the rest of his life there was between Alexander and the Macedonians a subdued tension, breaking out from time to time into bitter tragedies.

Of more immediate importance was a different trouble – also destined to dog Alexander for the rest of his life. The question nearest the heart of every average Macedonian soldier had already long been, 'When are we going home?' Not long after the death of Dareios a rumour swept through the camp that the war was over and the great day at hand. There was wild excitement; but when Alexander addressed a parade, pointing out that Bessos was still in arms, and explaining that if they did not consolidate what they had won, the East would forget them 'like a passing dream', the troops soon let themselves be rekindled to some semblance of enthusiasm. The episode had not been serious; but it was a straw in the wind.

Alexander established a field post office to assist the troops in writing home. It also assisted Alexander, by means of a secret censorship, to keep his finger on the state of morale.

Bessos in Bactria had assumed the upright *tiara* – the pointed cap which all men but the King wore soft and falling to one side – and, styling himself 'King Artaxerxes', was raising a cavalry army of Bactrians and 'Scythians'. Against him Alexander now marched; but before he had gone far serious news overtook him. Satibarzanes, repenting of his surrender, was raising Areia in revolt, and had massacred the handful of troops sent by Alexander to protect his people when the army was passing his borders.

Leaving Krateros to follow with the main army, Alexander swept south again with the Companions, mounted javelin-men, archers, Agriânes, and Koinos' and Amyntas' battalions. Covering seventy miles in two days, they reached Satibarzanes' capital, while his levies scattered to their homes in dismay. After a few days' savage hunting of the fugitives, while Krateros and the main body came up, Alexander, failing to catch Satibarzanes, marched on – no longer against Bessos, but south again into Helmund valley, the old Kingdom of Drangiana, which had been occupied by Barsaëntes. Now or later he gave orders for a city to be founded as a permanent post in Areia : Alexandria in Areia, still famous as Herat.

Barsaëntes, like Satibarzanes, was caught unready, and fled towards the Indus; but even here Alexander's shadow followed him. The Indians, from fear of the strange conqueror, arrested him and sent him in chains to Alexander, who put him to death for his crime against Dareios – though the contrast with Nabarzanes shows that what really weighed with Alexander was his 'rebellion'.

At the capital of Drangiana something far worse occurred.

It began when a young man named Dymnos conspired with 'persons unknown' against Alexander's life; possibly in favour of Alexander of Lynkestis, possibly merely from hysterical longing for an end of these forced marches. Dymnos tried to enlist for this design a youth named Nîkomachos, of whom he was very fond. Nîkomachos, horrified, though sworn to secrecy, told his elder brother Kebalinos; and Kebalinos reported the matter to Philôtas, asking for an audience with the King. But Philôtas said the King was busy.

The son of Parmenion was not a popular figure among Alexander's friends. He was a magnificent cavalry leader, whose dash and endurance vied with Alexander's own; but he was arrogant, conspicuous even among those others whose heads had been turned by sudden wealth, for reckless generosity and

tasteless magnificence; Parmenion himself had caustically advised him to 'be less of a hero'. He resented the King's successful
disregard of Parmenion's advice, and had already been reported
in Egypt for what might be construed as treasonable conversation; but Alexander, making allowances for the loose talk of a
great fighting man (and perhaps for the fact that his young
brother Hector had just been drowned in the Nile) let the matter
drop. Philôtas, however, remained an object of dislike and suspicion to the 'inner circle' – Hêphaistion, Krateros and even his
own brother-in-law Koinos; and Alexander was, in fact, receiving secret reports, through Krateros, of Philôtas' bragging to his
mistress, referring to Alexander as a mere boy, who owed
everything to the family of Parmenion. Philôtas' mistress was a
girl named Antigone, from Pydna; sold to a slave-dealer probably after Philip's capture of her town in her infancy, twenty-
three years before. Thence, via the harem of a Persian officer,
she had come into Philôtas' possession after Issos. Apparently
she did not love him either. And now Philôtas' remaining
brother, Nîkânor, commander of the footguards, had died of
sickness in Media, and Parmenion had been left on lines of
communication ever since what Alexander considered his
failure at Gaugamêla.

Kebalinos approached Philôtas again next day, but was still
put off. Whether Philôtas really thought the affair frivolous
never became clear; but Kebalinos, seriously worried, now
spoke to a youth nearer his own age, the page on duty at the
armoury. Now at least there was no delay. The page, with a
boy's impetuosity, hid Kebalinos in the armoury and went and
told Alexander in his bath. A squad was sent to fetch Dymnos;
but Dymnos drew his sword upon them, and was killed resisting arrest. His evidence was thus lost; but Philôtas' enemies
unanimously urged that a nonentity like Dymnos would never
have thought of such a design by himself; someone greater
must have been behind him. Alexander, seriously perturbed,
ordered the arrest of Philôtas. He was placed on trial before the
Macedonian army, representing the nation – the regular proce-
dure in treason trials, where the King was, as it were, a party in

the case. His defence was heard, and was traversed by Alexander. The damning fact was that Philôtas had heard of a plot against the King's life and had said nothing about it for two days, though, as commander of the horse-guards, he saw the King regularly, twice a day. He was found guilty and, according to Ptolemy (Arrian), killed on the spot by the troops with a shower of javelins, this also being the national custom in such trials. According to Curtius and Plutarch, he was first tortured for evidence, Krateros, Koinos and Hêphaistion themselves supervising, while Alexander listened, concealed behind a curtain; but of this Arrian says nothing.

After this, there was naturally a 'security panic'. Amyntas, son of Andromenes, was arrested with his brothers Simmias and Attalos. He had been a friend of Philôtas, and had likewise indulged in loose talk against Alexander. Also his third brother Polemon had fled in a panic after the arrest of Philôtas.

Amyntas, however, put up a stout defence, and successfully showed that there was nothing concrete against him. He had been a friend of Philôtas? Certainly. Queen Olympias had warned the King against him? Very likely. When he was recruiting in Macedonia last year, he had considered it his duty to round up shirkers wherever they might be found, and he had extracted some who had attached themselves to the Queen's household. No doubt these gentlemen had said their worst to her. He had been obstructive and insolent when a royal secretary came round commandeering officers' spare horses? Well, perhaps he had; but after all, he had once had ten horses, and the needs of the army had already reduced him to two. He was sorry, he was a bit too free with his tongue; but, 'You know what we soldiers are, King; we grumble one day, and we're ready to march to India the next.' As for that young brother of his – Amyntas requested leave of absence to go and look for him.

Alexander gave leave, and Amyntas went out into the mountains and brought his brother in, very much ashamed.

The acquittal of the sons of Andromenes suggests more than

anything else that Philôtas too received a genuine hearing before condemnation.

At the same time, Alexander ordered the execution of Alexander son of Aëropos, who was still in durance. If people were going to conspire, one must remove the alternative monarch. Also, though the victim was still Antipatros' son-in-law, the King had less cause to mind now about Antipatros' feelings.

There remained Parmenion. In two reigns he had always been the soul of loyalty, and he had already lost two sons in Alexander's war; but Alexander was not the man to let old services weigh against policy. In accordance with the old, savage Macedonian practice of killing the kindred in high-treason cases, he decided at once that Parmenion must die. A security cordon was cast round the camp to prevent any unauthorized person from leaving it; and Polydamas, a Companion, was sent with orders to Menidas, Sitalkes and Kleandros, Parmenion's three chief subordinates at the base at Ecbatana. Travelling with swift dromedaries, Polydamas covered the 400 miles in eleven days.

The old marshal was walking in a park that had belonged to the Persian kings when the three colonels and the messenger waited on him. They gave him a letter with the seal of the King, and another with that of his son, and as he was about to open them, the four of them cut him down.

There was a riot among his troops, who flatly refused to believe the official story that Parmenion had been killed for treason. At best there had been some hideous mistake. Kleandros and the others got them quiet at last and handed over the body for honourable burial. The head had to go to Alexander for identification. Alexander had the rioters drafted into a special battalion, to be kept apart from the main army; and such was his hold over his troops that they continued in this unit to serve him faithfully throughout his days. He also divided the horse-guards into two regiments, under Hêphaistion and Kleitos. Even his dearest friend should never be trusted in command of the whole of that great cavalry brigade again.

It was now autumn, but Alexander, probably feeling that the

state of morale rendered idleness dangerous, did not halt for the winter. His columns pushed southward as far as the harmless, primitive folk of Gedrosia, in Beluchistan, and back again through Arachosia, where a Macedonian, Menon – not an Asiatic – was left as Satrap. Here, also, Amyntas was killed attacking a hill fort. They halted once for long enough to found Alexandria-in-Arachosia (Kandahar), and again for an Alexander-under-Caucasus, near the headwaters of the River Kabul. The reverberations of the Philôtas affair still rumbled; during the winter one of the seven bodyguards, Dêmêtrios, was arrested in connection with it; in his stead was appointed Ptolemy son of Lagôs, the historian and later King. Marching again, often hungry, in snow and bitter cold, by early spring the army approached the high passes of the Hindu Kush, to invade Bactria from the south.

West of them Satibarzanes reappeared with 2,000 Bactrian cavalry, to raise Areia in revolt again; but Alexander, confident that the people had had a lesson, did not turn this time. He sent a force under Erigyios, with Artabazos as political adviser, and also ordered Phratapherenes to invade Areia from Parthia. Erigyios brought Satibarzanes to bay at last in a severe action, and killed him with his own hand, with the Macedonian lance-thrust in the face. Here also, having found two Persians wanting, Alexander now appointed a Greek governor, Stasânor, a prince of Cyprus.

'Artaxerxes' had wasted the valleys north of the Hindu Kush in the hope of stopping Alexander for lack of supplies; but in vain. Half-starved, floundering in deep snow on the pass, their horses dying, themselves living on mutton and wild silphium, the men went on. At last they reached easier country; Bessos, finding resistance hopeless, fled over the Oxus to the frontier province of Sogdiana, burning the river craft behind him, while his Bactrians scattered to their homes. Alexander occupied Bactra (Balkh), the capital, and installed old Artabazos as Satrap; moved on to the Oxus, where he dismissed to their homes a number of the older Macedonians and the Thessalians who had stayed with him so far; and, finding the country bare of timber,

got his army over the great river in five days on rafts made
of the leather bivouac tents stuffed with dry grass. Beyond the
river he remounted his cavalry with the horses of Turkestan.

Soon afterwards Bessos, betrayed by Spitamenes, the Sogdian leader, was captured by a flying-column under Ptolemy;
and Ptolemy wrote to ask how he should bring Bessos into
the King's presence. Alexander answered that he should stand
him bound and naked (itself a savage degradation to a Persian –
Persians did not strip for exercise) on the right of the road by
which the army would pass. Alexander reined in his chariot
and demanded, why had Bessos so treated Dareios, his King,
kinsman and benefactor? Bessos answered that what had been
done was done by common consent of Dareios' officers, hoping
thus to find favour with Alexander. Alexander then ordered
him to be scourged, while a herald stood by repeating the re-
proaches implied in Alexander's question. Then Bessos was sent
on to Bactra to be killed later, while Alexander advanced to the
Sogdian capital, Marakanda, which is Samarkand.

Here he received an embassy from the nomads towards the
Caspian and sent one in return, to swear friendship and – his
real motive – to gather topographical, economic and military
intelligence. He himself moved on to the Iaxartes (Syr Darya),
where he planned to found another Alexandria, known later as
'Alexandria at the End of the World' (Eschate) – today Khodjend.

Near Khodjend, he was badly wounded in the leg by an
arrow, breaking the fibula, while storming a mountain fortress
whose inhabitants had cut off some of his foragers.

Bactria had fallen easily, but the warlike frontier province
was a different story. The signs of a permanent Greek occupation roused the latent national feeling; and when Alexander
summoned all chiefs to a durbar at Zariaspa (the Persian name
of Bactra), Spitamenes and others placed themselves at its
head. The savage treatment of Bessos had evidently done no
good. Revolt flared up along the Syr Darya, and the small

garrisons in the towns among the irrigated gardens were suddenly attacked and massacred. The rebellion spread to Bactria, and Spitamenes rode with his cavalry to attack Samarkand.

Alexander sent Krateros to besiege the largest riverside town, a fortress founded by Cyrus. With the rest of his army he stormed the low mud walls of three 'towns' in two days, slaughtering men and enslaving the women and children. From two more towns the inhabitants fled, and were cut down in thousands by Alexander's cavalry, whom, guessing that this would happen, he had sent ahead to catch them. Then he stormed 'Cyrus' City', a tougher proposition, personally leading a party – though he must have been still lame – up a dry torrent bed and under the water-gate, while Krateros assaulted the walls. Krateros was wounded by an arrow, and Alexander was struck on the side of the head by a stone, damaging his sight for some time. But the city was taken.

Meanwhile the 'Scythians' were gathering in hordes beyond the river, scenting a chance to break into the settled lands. Alexander kept his main army facing them, while detaching some 2,300 mercenaries, of whom 800 were mounted, and sixty Companions, all under his interpreter Pharnouches the Lykian, as 'political officer', to deal with Spitamenes' westward raid. He was anxious to teach the nomads a lesson.

In three weeks the new Alexandria had a defensible wall, and was solemnly inaugurated with the usual prayers and sports. Its population consisted of some of the older mercenaries and Macedonians, left as a garrison, and of voluntarily recruited natives. But the omens for crossing the river were not favourable.

After chafing for some time, Alexander decided to defy the omens. His field artillery, shooting across the river, scared away the nomads from the bank, especially after a mounted chief had fallen, pierced clean through his leather shield and scale-armour by a feathered javelin at several hundred yards; and to the sound of the trumpet Alexander personally led over, on the usual rafts of bivouac tents, first his archers and slingers, then armoured infantry, then his cavalry. A first charge by the lancers was met by the immemorial encircling tactics of the Steppe – the tactics of mounted men rounding up cattle. The lancers and mercenary cavalry could not get near their enemies, who followed and shot at them when they turned back. Alexander, taking in the problem at a glance, then drew up a mixed line of cavalry and light infantry with missile weapons (a foot-archer can outrange a horse-archer, since he can carry a longer bow). The nomads, puzzled, must then have 'bunched' unwisely; for a sudden charge of heavy cavalry got in among them, and routed them with the loss of 1,000 killed and 150 prisoners. Alexander pursued for a long way in the summer heat, and came back with a bad attack of dysentery from drinking surface water.

The local nomad king sued for peace. The projected raid into the settled lands, he said, had been a piece of indiscipline on the part of some of his young men. Alexander decided to 'believe' this story, in order to turn against Spitamenes; for that chieftain, after being stoutly repulsed by the garrison of Samarkand, had turned against the relieving column and, chiefly by the aid of 600 nomad horse-archers, destroyed it to a man.

It was a painful story : the ambush; the usual difficulties of dealing with 'Parthian' tactics; the exhausting, baffled advance; the weary retreat in hollow square, with many wounded and the enemy growing bolder; altercation among the officers, with Pharnouches trying to resign his command to the soldier Andromachos, and Andromachos refusing; the intention to take cover in a river bed; the cavalry hurrying ahead to get to it; the infantry, scenting betrayal, hurrying, breaking into a run; and a massacre in the wadi. It was the bloodiest, and the only serious, defeat ever suffered by one of Alexander's columns.

Spitamenes returned and renewed the blockade of Samarkand; but Alexander himself was now marching to the rescue. Covering 170 miles in three days and three nights, the indomitable 'Archers, Agriânes, Foot-Guards and lightest of the Phalanx', with the Companion cavalry, arrived at dawn; but Spitamenes and his horsemen had vanished. It only remained to conduct fierce reprisals on the villages that had supported him, to bury the dead of the lost column, and then to take up quarters at Zariaspa for the winter.

Iran was still not finished.

At Zariaspa drafts arrived, both of Europeans and Asiatics. The mission sent to the Caspian also returned, with a further embassy from a new King of the Scyths, offering the hand of his daughter, and with Pharasmanes, King of Chorasmia, in person, offering to guide Alexander against – so the Macedonians understood – the Amazons and the land of the Golden Fleece. From these missions a legend grew up, quickly enough to be laughed at by some of Alexander's own officers before they died, that the Queen of the Amazons herself had ridden untold miles for the purpose of having a child by Alexander. The Alexander-mythology was already in the making.

Alexander also conducted a 'trial' of Bessos, before such Persian nobles as were with him: Artabazos, Phrataphernes (who had meanwhile captured Bessos' Satrap of Parthia), Bessos of Syria and others. Bessos' nose and ears were cut off and he was sent on to Ectabana to be put to death by a general council of the Medes and Persians.

The King was certainly learning the ways of Persia. It was also during this winter that he made a systematic effort to get his Macedonians to prostrate themselves before him in the Persian manner. The Macedonians did not take kindly to the idea at all; the gallant body-guard Leonnâtos was temporarily under a cloud for laughing when he saw Persians doing it; and both Macedonians and 'other' Greeks – since in Greece one bowed down before gods and not before men – mixed up this question with that of Alexander's divinity, his claim to which was being enthusiastically urged by the courtier-philosopher Anaxarchos.[1]

A cunning effort was made to introduce this 'kow-tow' at a state banquet, apparently in the hope that politeness would

1. Anaxarchos, a sinister figure in the Alexander story, may have been authoritarian by conviction – like his contemporaries, the Legalist philosophers of China. He got into trouble himself after Alexander's death, and died very bravely.

prevent any unfortunate incidents. Each guest, Macedonian, Greek or Persian in succession, was invited to drink from the King's cup, and thereafter to exchange the kiss of friendship with the King – another Persian custom. But first, each guest was expected to make obeisance.

All went well up to a point. The example set not only by Persians but by carefully selected Macedonians, such as the faithful Hêphaistion, was followed by several others. But then came a hitch. Kallisthenes, feeling that as a philosopher he must assert his conscientious objections, approached, deliberately omitting the prostration. Alexander was looking the other way, talking to Hêphaistion, and did not notice; but somebody else called out, 'He has not made obeisance!' Alexander thereupon refused to kiss Kallisthenes, who withdrew unabashed, remarking, 'Well, then, I retire – the poorer by a kiss!'

Seeing the strength of Macedonian feeling, Alexander ultimately abandoned the project; but he bore a grudge against Kallisthenes. Kallisthenes in general was losing ground to Anaxarchos, partly by his own fault. He was growing arrogant and tiresome. A philosopher, he was untouched by the effects of wealth upon a Philôtas or a Leonnâtos; but, more subtly, perhaps, yet no less certainly, he was giving way to pride. He had been heard to remark, for example, that others might have joined Alexander to win glory for themselves, but he, the historian, had come to confer it on Alexander. Anaxarchos, on the other hand, while as a professional philosopher he affected the direct and uncourtly speech of a Diogenes, was systematically currying favour by encouraging the King in his tendency towards absolutism.

While the question of the obeisance was still alive, another episode occurred, which shook Alexander's pride more than any other in his career. Alexander, abstemious in his youth, was drinking more and more heavily, and at a banquet on a feast of the Dioskouroi, the deified heroes Kastor and Polydeukes, a tragedy occurred.

The now usual flattery was going on. Anaxarchos asked, what were the deeds of the Dioskouroi in comparison with Alexander's, that they should be regarded as children of Zeus rather than of their earthly father, Tyndareus? Why should the envy of men forbid the great to be honoured as divine until they were dead?

As to what happened then, accounts differ in details, as those of eyewitnesses remembering the scene afterwards well might. But it appears that Black Kleitos, some distance from Alexander, began reciting to those near him some lines from Euripides' *Andromache* – a play referring to the ancestors of Olympias' family, which had no doubt been played more than once at Alexander's dramatic festivals:

> Alas, in Greece how ill the custom runs!
> The trophies stand inscribed with names of kings;
> – The blood that won the field was other men's!

All accounts agree that Kleitos, however good his cause, was rude and 'asked for trouble'. Alexander, without losing his temper, told him to leave the hall; but Kleitos was at the obstinate stage of drunkenness, and broke out into an angry protest against some allusion, in a new poem which had just been sung, to the Macedonians who had been defeated in Alexander's absence. Macedonians, he grumbled, were better men than these Persians here, even if they had met with misfortune.

'You are pleading your own cause, Kleitos,' said Alexander, 'when you call misconduct misfortune.'

Kleitos sprang to his feet, waving his hand. 'Yet it was my conduct and this right hand,' he shouted, 'that saved you, you "son of the gods", from getting Spithridates' sword in your back! And it is by the blood of Macedonians and by these wounds of ours that you have grown so great as to make yourself the son of Amon and disown Philip!'

'Do you imagine,' cried Alexander, 'that you can go on talking like this at all times and making trouble among the Macedonians, and not be sorry for it?'

'We are sorry already,' said Kleitos. 'We envy the dead who did not live to see Macedonians beaten with Median rods and asking Persians as a favour for an audience with the King.'

Men near Alexander were on their feet now answering Kleitos, while the older men tried to quiet the rising tumult. Alexander said quietly to two Greeks who were near him, 'Do you not feel that Greeks walk among Macedonians like demi-gods among beasts?'

But Kleitos, resisting attempts to suppress him, was still shouting, 'Speak up, King! Tell us all! – or else don't invite free-spoken men to dinner, confine yourself to your kow-towing Persian slaves!' Alexander lost his temper at last, threw an apple at Kleitos with unerring aim and reached for his sword; but one of the body-guards had had the presence of mind to remove it. His friends crowded round him, trying to quiet him, but Alexander, in a raging fury at being thwarted, shouted in rough Macedonian for the guards to turn out, and bade the trumpeter sound the alarm. The trumpeter had the nerve to disobey, and Alexander struck him, crying that he was in the plight of Dareios, put under arrest by his own people, King only in name. Meanwhile Ptolemy and others pushed Kleitos, still shouting, out of the hall.

Everyone breathed again.

But Kleitos, in the open air, broke loose. His voice was heard outside the curtain covering another doorway. Then the curtain was torn aside. Kleitos stood there, crying, 'Here I am, Alexander!'

Alexander snatched a pike from a guard and ran him through the body. Kleitos fell with a groan and died almost at once.

Alexander's rage vanished in a moment. He pulled out the bloody pike and tried to turn its butt to the wall, to throw himself on its point; but his friends prevented him, and he let them lead him away, groaning. 'Oh, Kleitos, Kleitos, ill have I repaid you! Ill have I requited Lânîke's fostering, and her sons who fell in my battles!'

In his quarters he lay for three days without wine or food, in an agony of shame, before he let the seers persuade him to sacrifice to the Wine-God Dionysos, whose anger had caused the tragedy; for the day had been a feast of Dionysos too, it appeared, and while they sacrificed to the Dioskouroi, the offering to him had been omitted.

The philosopher 'chaplains' also tried to console him; but Kallisthenes' rationalist palliations and reminders of how greatly he had been provoked gave him little comfort. Anaxarchos' methods had more success, when, finding the King lying speechless, he laughed brutally and cried, 'This, then, is Alexander, the Lord of the World! He lies weeping like a slave for fear of the law and censure of men, to whom he himself should be a law! Do you not know the meaning of that saying, that Justice sits at the right hand of God? It means, that whatever is ordained by God, is rightly done; and so too on earth, what has been done by the King must be thought just, first of all by the King himself, and secondly by the rest of men.'

By this appeal to Alexander's absolutism, Anaxarchos appeased at least that part of his remorse which was based on the last relics of his respect for Macedonian opinion.

Action was the best anodyne, and there was still need of it. Spitamenes was still at large and Sogdiana still unsubdued. In 328, leaving Krateros in Bactria with a large force, including two-thirds of the phalanx, Alexander combed the country with five columns, four respectively under Koinos (with Artabazos), Hêphaistion, Ptolemy and Perdikkas, while he himself, with the fifth, took the road from Bactra to Samarkand. At Samarkand the columns reunited, and he then sent Koinos and Artabazos to raid the independent nomads, among whom Spitamenes was reported, and Hêphaistion to unite the villages of Sogdiana into walled towns – i.e. to concentrate the population, so that they could not easily help the guerrillas. The campaign becomes more and more reminiscent of the hunting of De Wet. Alexander himself captured stronghold after stronghold where the 'rebels' still attempted defence. Meanwhile, however, Spitamenes, with 600 nomads and his Sogdian diehards, once more broke back south into Bactria, destroying a minor garrison and raiding up to Zariaspa. At this base there was a hospital and convalescent depot, and the officer in command there, with some convalescent horse-guardsmen and about eighty Greek troopers of the garrison, by a bold sortie, routed the Scythians as they were driving off plunder; but Spitamenes caught them returning, killing seven Companions and sixty of the eighty Greeks. Krateros pursued Spitamenes and inflicted some losses; but the main body of the nomads once more vanished into the steppe.

This year Alexander left Koinos to winter in Sogdiana, with two battalions of the phalanx, 400 Companion cavalry, the mounted javelin-men and most of the friendly Sogdian and Bactrian cavalry which had now been organized, with orders to waylay Spitamenes if he should reappear.

Sure enough, Spitamenes came again in the winter with 3,000 horse. But they found the countryside swept bare; all people and all supplies had been gathered within the walls of Hêphaistion's new 'cities', under guard of Greek or Macedonian garrisons. In desperation they turned against Koinos, and sustained a bloody defeat, losing 800 killed; the Macedonians lost twenty-five cavalry killed, and twelve infantry. Spitamenes fell back in his last and grimmest retreat. His Sogdian and Bactrian cavalry, ragged and half-starved, melted away, deserting by hundreds to surrender to Koinos. The Scythians, grown surly with defeat, looted the pack-horse baggage train of those who were left. Spitamenes rode on in the freezing wind, with these savage allies, having, indeed, little choice. Then the Scythians heard a report that Alexander himself was preparing to pursue them. They cut off Spitamenes' head and sent it to the King.

So died Alexander's most redoubtable opponent. The troops were now able to spend the worst of the winter under cover at Nautaka (Bokhara?), while Alexander attended to administration: receiving Stasânor and Phrataphernes to report on their year's work; ordering the former to take over the Helmund valley (Drangiana), and the latter to arrest Autophradates of Mardia, who, though repeatedly summoned, had not come to report. Mazaios, at Babylon, had died, and was replaced by Harpalos, who also kept the post of Lord Treasurer; and Artabazos in Bactria, after three years' continuous hard work, resigned on grounds of age. No other Iranian could be trusted with this vital post, and a Macedonian, Amyntas, son of Nîkolaos, was appointed. Alexander also superseded, as suspect, Oxodates of Media, appointing one Atropates, whose name was destined to stick to the province for over 2,000 years (Atropatêne = Azerbaijan).

Early in 327 Alexander broke camp, still to 'finish off' Sogdiana, and laid siege to a reputedly impregnable fortress, the Sogdian Rock, probably in what is still called the Hissar (= the Fortress) Range. In it many of the guerrilla fighters still in arms, including Oxyartes, a Bactrian leader who had been with Bessos, had left their families for safety, while they kept up the guerrilla war. It was amply provisioned, and the defenders laughed at Alexander's summons to surrender, bidding him look for winged soldiers, for no others could come up there.

Alexander called for volunteers 'who had practised rock-climbing in the various sieges', and offered rewards of 300 gold pieces each for the first 300 men to climb the cliff, with special prizes for the leaders, rising to twelve talents – a considerable fortune – for the first man of all. There was a rush to volunteer, and that very night they tackled a peak overlooking the fort, so formidable that it was unguarded, working methodically with ropes and their iron tent-pegs, which they drove as *pitons* into crannies or into the frozen snow. No less than thirty men fell, 'so that not even their bodies were found for burial, where they fell in the snow'; but by dawn the remainder were up, still unobserved, and signalled to Alexander. Alexander then sent a second herald to repeat the summons to surrender quickly while there was time – 'for the King had found his airborne soldiers'. And with that, the rock-climbers on the pinnacle stood up on the skyline and showed themselves.

They were only 270 and sketchily armed, but the defenders did not know that. They surrendered hastily, and it was not necessary to send reinforcements up the fixed ropes.

Among the families of the guerrilla warriors captured here was a young girl of especial beauty, Roxâne, daughter of the brave Oxyartes. Alexander, seeing her, fell deeply in love,[1] perhaps for the first time in his life; but he would not simply take her as a captive. His chivalry was rewarded, for not long after, Oxyartes came in and surrendered. A few weeks later Alexander and Roxâne were married, by the Iranian ceremony, whose central rite was the eating together of a wheaten cake, cut by the bridegroom. Alexander, on one of his impulses, added a symbolic detail and cut the cake with his sword.

First, however, he marched on, Oxyartes with him, into the last north-eastern corner of the Empire, Paraitakêne, whose mountain ranges stretched up to Pamir. Here, too, there was an 'impregnable' fortress, the Rock of Khoriênes.

'Is the king of it a fighting man?' asked Alexander of Oxyartes.

'He is not,' said Oxyartes.

'Then it doesn't matter what his fortress is like,' said Alexander.

The fortress was cut off from the main mountain mass by a deep ravine, and a rock-climbing surprise could not be attempted twice. Setting his men to cut logs in the dense fir forest, Alexander started to build a causeway. Ladders had first to be made and fixed to the near slope, so that the workers could get down. By day he himself supervised the work, with half the army employed, and by night Perdikkas and Leonnâtos and Ptolemy with the remainder, in three shifts. In a day they advanced barely ten yards and in a night rather less, so difficult was the ground. Snow fell, and the army suffered from bitter winds and lack of supplies, but the work went on, while mantlets kept off missiles from above. Presently arrows from the causeway began to reach the walls; and then the chief sent a herald asking that Oxyartes might be sent to parley. Oxyartes went, and after he had suitably praised Alexander as invincible and as chivalrous, the Rock surrendered. Alexander accepted its

1. So Plutarch says. Tarn, in view of Alexander's usual sexual coldness, would doubt even this romantic story; he considers the match a successful stroke of policy, to conciliate the frontier barons.

chief as his vassal, and governor of his old domains, and while Krateros, in a fierce battle, crushed the last two independent chiefs in Paraitakêne, the main army, amply provisioned from the Rock's vast supplies, returned to Bactria en route for India. It was still only spring.

But he was not to leave Iran without one more tragedy. Among the royal pages there was one Hermolâos, spirited, promising and something of an intellectual – a favourite pupil of Kallisthenes. At a boar-hunt near Bactra, he so far forgot himself as to shoot before the King, and the boar fell. Alexander, like the Oriental monarch that he had become, was furious, ordered Hermolâos to be flogged in the presence of the other pages and deprived him of his horse. Smarting physically and mentally, Hermolâos complained to his particular friend, that he could not live unless he avenged the insult. Tyrannicide was, by the tenets of all Greek philosophy, including Aristotle's, a virtuous act, and the boys had heard of the Athenian heroes Harmodios and Aristogeiton long before Alexander turned into the traditional monster before their eyes. Other boys were sounded, and joined in – one of them the son of Asklêpiodôros, late Governor of Syria. This boy's turn on night duty at Alexander's quarters was due shortly, and on that night they determined to kill him in his sleep.

But Alexander happened to sit up drinking all that night – urged to do so, according to Aristoboulos, by a Syrian prophetess, whose warnings had repeatedly proved curiously sound; and next day, in the usual manner, the plot leaked out. One of the boys told a former admirer of his; the latter, worried, told the boy's elder brother and the brother reported the whole thing, with names, to Ptolemy. Alexander ordered the arrest of all those named, and on the rack the boys confessed their conspiracy and added a few names more. They were then tried for treason before the army. Hermolâos is said to have confessed boldly that he had plotted to liberate all from the tyrant, the Oriental despot, the drunkard, the slayer of Philôtas, Parmenion. Kleitos – and so on till a hail of stones from the army silenced him for ever.

At the same time Kallisthenes was arrested. Some of the boys are said to have confessed under torture that he had encouraged them to conspire. Such evidence would be worth little; but Kallisthenes' political philosophy was, at bottom, the republicanism of the city-state; it was beyond gainsaying that Hermolâos had been attached to him. As a man of Olynthos he was both a Greek citizen and a Macedonian subject (there were Chalkidian squadrons among the Companions), so that he could, *pace* some modern writers, have been tried before the army. One of the boys who were tried was the son of a Thracian chief. That he was not so tried probably indicates that there was no serious case against him. But it was evident that his ideals and Alexander's monarchy were no longer compatible. Ptolemy, who should have known, and who was inclined on the whole to whitewash Alexander, said that he was tortured and crucified; Aristoboulos, that he was carried with the army as a prisoner for a long time and ultimately died (of typhus?), filthy, lousy and bloated. It would seem that he must have disappeared from human ken into a sinister silence; a martyr, whatever his faults, for rationalism and freedom of speech.

11 Indian Summers
   (327–5)

Crossing the Hindu Kush in ten days, Alexander reached Alexandria-under-Caucasus and superseded the Governor as inadequate. Ever since 330 he had had the Indian expedition in mind, and he was already in touch with the Rajah of Taxila on the Indus, who, as he was getting the worst of things in his wars with the redoubtable Paurava Rajah beyond the Jhelum, was prepared to welcome Alexander.

Sending Hêphaistion and Perdikkas ahead by the Kabul valley with half the phalanx and most of the cavalry, to prepare pontoons and build boats on the Indus, Alexander, with his usual mobile force, fought his way through the mountains north of it, to 'pacify' that formidable hill-country. Resistance was fierce; at one 'city' Alexander, Leonnâtos and Ptolemy were all slightly wounded; at another place Ptolemy, in command of a column, felled an Indian king in single combat, throwing his spear when he found that the Indian's pike was longer, while his armour saved him from the Indian's thrust; and there was then a 'Homeric' battle over the corpse. Fiercest of all was the fighting at Aornos, a mountain stronghold several miles in circumference, where Ptolemy, having seized by surprise a vantage point at the far end of the fortress, was cut off there for two days and hard pressed before the main body could break through to him. There was a legend that a mythical hero, whom the Greeks identified with their Hêrakles, had been unable to take Aornos, and Alexander was particularly proud of having succeeded where his great ancestor had failed. Not till the next spring (326) was the army reunited on the Indus, somewhere near Attock.

It was a new world into which they were penetrating, and it made a vivid impression on the Greek imagination: the teeming population, the dark faces ('the Indians are the darkest of mankind except the Ethiopians,' writes Arrian); the great rivers, the cities, the fakirs, whom they called the 'naked philosophers', the elephants, the crocodiles – then found in the Indus. Alexander knew something of the politics of the Punjab, but he knew nothing whatever of what lay to southward, and when he saw crocodiles in the Indus his first thought was that these were the headwaters of the Nile. The invaders did not grasp the caste system, but they saw the activities of the warrior Kshattriya, whom they supposed to be mercenaries, after the Greek manner, and of the Brahmans, 'the philosophers of the Indians', whose unbending nationalism made them Alexander's sternest opponents. Buddhism is not mentioned, but the 'naked philosophers' may have been of the Jain religion.

Alexander was interested in the ascetics, as he had been formerly in Diogenes, 'marvelling at their endurance'; but they regarded him as might have been expected. A story is told (by Arrian) of some of them stamping their feet when the King, with a large escort, visited them. 'Alexander asked by interpreters what this meant; and they replied: "O King Alexander, every man occupies so much earth as this, on which we step. You, who are a man like others (saving that you are restless and wanton), now pass over all this distance more, away from your own place, troubling yourself and other men; but in a little while when you are dead you will occupy just so much space as is enough to be buried in." '

'And Alexander praised the speech and the speakers, but he went on doing the opposite to that which he praised.'

Later he tried to get an ascetic to join his entourage; 'but the eldest of the school, named Dandamis, whose disciples the others were, said that he would not come, nor would he let the others; for if Alexander was the son of God, so was he himself; he had no need of anything that Alexander could give him, for he was well as he was; and moreover he saw Alexander's men wandering over all this land and sea to no good end, and finding no term of their wanderings ... Nor yet did he fear that Alexander could deprive him of anything that he needed; for in life the land of India was enough for him, producing its fruits in due season; and when he died, he would be well rid of the body as of an ill companion.'

One of the school, however, whom the Greeks called Kalanos, decided to follow Alexander; 'and the other philosophers reviled him'. This Kalanos later fell ill, for the first time in his life, in Persia, but refused treatment, 'saying to Alexander that it was better for him to die as he was, before he experienced an evil that should make him change his manner of life.' He therefore proposed to immolate himself. Alexander, after long efforts to persuade him to live, commissioned Ptolemy to do all that he asked. A pyre was piled up for him; the army paraded in his honour; and Kalanos, unable to walk or ride, 'was borne past on a litter, garlanded in the Indian manner and singing in the Indian tongue; the Indians say that these songs are hymns to the gods. So he mounted the pyre, and disposed himself, before the eyes of the host. Alexander felt that it was a horrible sight, the man being his friend; but the others marvelled, how he did not move at all in the fire. And when they lit the pyre, Nearchos says that the trumpets sounded, as Alexander had ordered, and the army shouted as they shouted when going into battle, and the elephants trumpeted as for war, shrilly, doing honour to Kalanos.'

Now, however, Alexander marched against Pôros, as the Greeks called the Paurava Rajah.

Time and chance had wrought many changes in the army that had crossed the Hellespont eight years before. Parmenion, Philôtas and Nîkânor were dead, and of the old phalanx colonels, Ptolemaios and Amyntas. Erigyios, too, was dead, of sickness in Bactria. Koinos and Krateros are now the two chief marshals; Perdikkas, a body-guard and commander of a regiment of the horse-guards (in place of Black Kleitos). Meleagros alone of the original six remains a phalanx colonel, unpromoted and probably nursing a grievance. The men famous later as the great successors of Alexander are coming to the front:

Perdikkas, Ptolemy, Lysimachos, later King of Thrace, now also a body-guard, and Seleukos 'the Conqueror', now commanding the foot-guards. Eumenes the Scribe has become Secretary of State, and is sometimes given an independent command, in which he shows high capacity; Hêphaistion is jealous of him, and of Krateros. The archers are under Tauron, their fourth colonel in ten years. In the ranks, the drafts brought in time and again by Menidas and others (Menidas has been chiefly a recruiting officer since his wound at Gaugamêla) have kept the Macedonian units filled up in spite of casualties and super-annuation; but most of the Greek mercenary infantry, also con-stantly supplemented by drafts, has been left on lines of com-munication, to garrison the dozens of new cities founded, especially in the warlike east of the Empire. In their place, Alexander has increased his striking power by recruiting thou-sands of the fine Iranian cavalry : Bactrians, Sogdians, Aracho-sians, and especially useful, 'Scythian' horse-archers. All of these, incidentally, while serving under Alexander, were hostages for the good behaviour of their tribes.

Nevertheless, it is still recognizably the old Macedonian army, plus additional cavalry. 'The archers and the Agriânes and the Hypaspistai' still form the 'light division', almost continuously employed. The units mentioned do not suggest a total strength of more than the old figure, about 40,000, in addition to 5,000 Indians under the King of Taxila. If the columns that invaded India numbered anything like the 120,000 believed in by some modern writers, the figure probably includes the numerous 'camp-followers' – muleteers, camel-drivers, doctors, pedlars, entertainers, women, etcetera – who accompanied the army.

Pôros stood on the Jhelum, with some 4,000 cavalry, 30,000 foot, some chariotry and (it is said) 200 elephants – probably an exaggeration. For the first time Alexander was faced by a deliberate attempt to hold a strong river line. The river, swollen by melting snow from the Himalayas, ran swiftly, filling its wide bed, a formidable obstacle, and the Paurava, a giant, six feet nine inches in height, was also a skilful and determined soldier.

Alexander sent Koinos back to bring the Indus flotilla overland in pieces. Launching it again on the Jhelum, he tested the defence by marching up and down to suitable crossing-places. The results were negative. Pôros had watchers and detachments at all suitable points, and his main army, including the elephants, proved capable of arriving anywhere in time to frustrate a crossing. There could be no question of forcing a landing by frontal assault, especially since Alexander's horses would not face the elephants. He had by now acquired a considerable number of elephants himself, but never used them in battle, probably for this reason. At the mere sight of the monsters on the bank, and at the sound of their trumpeting, the horses would become unmanageable and jump off the rafts which he had prepared to transport them.

His strategy in this situation bears comparison with that of the Allies on the English Channel in 1944.

He gave it out publicly that he intended to force the river, and if necessary would wait there till next winter, when it would, in places, be fordable. He collected corn sufficient for a long halt; and meanwhile he kept his flotilla and his army, divided into several detachments, in ceaseless movement, continually threatening this point and that, both by day and by noisy night alarms, and forcing Pôros to conform to his movements. Thus he gradually wore down to some extent the enemy's alertness. The monsoon came, and the rains, impeding movement; and Pôros, keeping vedettes posted along some fifty miles of bank, ceased to move his main forces in answer to threats.

Meanwhile Alexander selected the point for his real crossing. Seventeen miles upstream from his main camp the river had swung to its left in a huge meander, and then cut through, leaving a promontory on Alexander's bank and an island in midstream. The island and both banks were covered with dense jungle, and here Alexander had secretly brought up and hidden a considerable number of boats. The final preparations and the start of the crossing would be hidden by the island.

Open (and genuine) preparations for a crossing continued at

the main camp. Then, on a night of thunder and torrential rain, Alexander marched upstream, leaving Krateros in camp with two regiments of the phalanx, the 5,000 Indians, and the cavalry from Afghanistan, and with orders to attempt the crossing only if he saw that the bulk of Pôros' army, and especially the elephants, had gone.

Before reaching the crossing-place, and opposite the region where he expected to meet Pôros, he dropped three more regiments of the phalanx and the Greek mercenary cavalry, with orders to cross at several points when they saw the enemy fully committed to battle. As his own striking force, he had the foot-guards, archers, Agriânes, Koinos' old phalanx-regiment, now under 'White' Kleitos, the horse-guards, 'Dêmêtrios' Regiment' (perhaps the old lancers), his Bactrian and Sogdian cavalry, and the nomad horse-archers; in all 11,000 men, of whom 5,000 were mounted.

The boats and rafts were launched in the dark, and the troops, who had covered seventeen miles in mud, darkness and streaming rain, were ready to cross at first light. As they cleared the island, the Indian vedettes saw them and riders sped south to warn Pôros.

Speed was now everything. The cavalry landed, Alexander first of all, and pushed inland – only to find, as a further relic of the river's old meanderings, that yet another backwater still separated them from the farther shore. It was not wide, but after the night's rain it was over six feet deep. The entire movement seemed to have miscarried ... Then, after frantic searching, a ford was found and the leading units crossed, 'the men breast high and the horses with only their heads out' (evidence on the size of Alexander's mainly Bactrian horses) – just in time to form a front against the first Indian troops, 1,000 cavalry and sixty chariots (probably carrying archers, as in the old Indian epics), under Pôros' son. Against these Alexander loosed the horse-archers, followed by the heavy cavalry, and the Indians were swiftly routed; the young Paurava was killed with 400 of his men, and all the chariots, running heavily in the mud, captured in their retreat.

Meanwhile Pôros, leaving a detachment with a few elephants facing Krateros, had drawn up his main army on a stretch of sandy ground, to avoid the mud. The most modest estimate gives him 2,000 cavalry and 20,000 infantry; Arrian, 4,000 and 30,000. He drew up these in a single line, cavalry on the flanks, with chariots in front of the cavalry and the elephants – spaced out at regular intervals – in front of his centre. To close with such a centre would have been highly dangerous. Alexander, as usual, struck at the enemy's left wing.

Pôros' formation, in fact, lacked flexibility in face of his far more mobile enemy. Alexander, sending two cavalry regiments (1,000 lances?) under Koinos to threaten the enemy's right, moved his main force – horse-archers, then heavy cavalry, then foot-archers, then armoured infantry, and lastly the Agriânes – rapidly against the Indians' left flank. Pôros ordered his left-wing cavalry to move farther to the left to meet the outflanking threat, and those from his own right to reinforce his left; but Alexander had anticipated this, and Koinos had his orders, to follow them at a distance and to charge as soon as they tried to unite against Alexander. The result was a cavalry *mêlée* at a little distance from the infantry, with the Indians in a single mass, caught between Alexander and Koinos, forced to form a front in both directions, and trying to re-form under a rain of arrows, to which they could make no reply. Outnumbered and outmanoeuvred, they broke without even awaiting Alexander's charge, and fled to the shelter of the elephants, now moving up in support.

The Macedonian infantry, whom Alexander had ordered not to close until the enemy's cavalry was beaten, now came in, 'shooting at the mahouts and attacking the beasts themselves from every side'. The action was severe beyond anything in their previous experience, for the beasts broke into the serried ranks even of the phalanx, while the Indian cavalry, with fine courage, rallied and charged again at Alexander's, only to be flung back again upon the elephants, hopelessly outclassed. The whole of Alexander's cavalry was now formed in a single mass on the right of his infantry, and the whole line formed a crescent facing inward upon Pôros' original left flank, infantry engaging the elephants, while Alexander's cavalry, having completely turned the flank, had no elephants before them.

Pôros' infantry moved bravely up to join in the fighting; but to change front with precision in the middle of the battle was beyond their powers. It was a deep, narrow-fronted, increasingly shapeless mass that surged up against the deadly crescent enveloping their original left. Alexander's cavalry charged them again and again, working terrible havoc, while his infantry held grimly on, giving ground when necessary, against the dense, confused, but still formidable mass of Indian infantry, cavalry and elephants.

The elephants', says Arrian, 'now pent in a narrow space, did as much harm to friend as to foe. Most of the mahouts had been picked off by now; and the beasts, some of them wounded, others frightened and riderless, attacked friend and foe alike, pushing, trampling and killing. The Macedonians, however, having space to manoeuvre in, and attacking the beasts as they chose, gave ground when they attacked, and pressed after them, shooting at them, when they turned away; while the Indians, packed together, now suffered more. At last the exhausted beasts ceased to charge, but merely trumpeted and drew back, like ships backing water; and Alexander, enveloping the whole mass of the Indians with his cavalry, and bidding the infantry close up their ranks to the uttermost, signalled to the phalanx [1] to advance. The Indian cavalry were almost entirely cut to pieces; their infantry were going down before the attacks of the Macedonians on every side; and the whole army broke and fled in the one direction that Alexander's cavalry left open.'

The rout was very bloody, for Krateros had by now forced the river-crossing, and his fresh troops took up the pursuit. Alexander had lost 310 men killed, of whom 230 were cavalry.

Pôros himself fought to the last, but, try as he would, he could not redeploy his line and make his numbers tell, in face

1. Presumably the three phalanx regiments which had been left with orders to cross during the battle. Arrian never mentions them again.

of the enemy's superiority in cavalry and archers and the
deadly skirmishing tactics of the Agriânes. Two of his sons, his
cavalry commanders, nearly all his chief officers and the governor of the Jhelum province fell fighting. At last, when all was
lost, bleeding from a wound in the right shoulder, on which he
wore no armour, he turned his elephant and rode off. Alexander sent the Rajah of Taxila after him to get into touch with
him; but even now, at the sight of his old enemy, the Paurava
turned his elephant again and charged, causing 'Taxiles', who
was on horseback, to ride for his life. Alexander then sent
other Indians, including an old friend of Pôros. Pôros at last
halted, bade his elephant set him down, and after a drink and a
breathing-space bade them bring him to Alexander.

'Ask him what he would like,' said Alexander.

'To be treated like a king,' said Pôros.

'Certainly,' said Alexander. 'But what would you like personally?'

'"As a king" covers everything,' was the answer.

This was a man after Alexander's heart. He confirmed him in
his kingdom, and with Alexandrian generosity subsequently
added further territory, whose inhabitants had hitherto managed to remain independent. He founded a city, Nikaia, the
'City of Victory', at the scene of the battle, and another at the
crossing of the Jhelum, called Boukephala, after the horse
Boukephalas, which died soon after the battle at a green old
age.

Organizing the territory as he went, he marched on, crossing
the Chenab and the Ravi, storming yet more cities, his appetite
whetted by what he now heard of India beyond the Sutlej: a
stretch of arid country, and then another great river, the Ganges,
its banks lined with great civilized kingdoms, flowing to the
eastern sea.

The troops had heard of the Ganges kingdoms too. Their
united military strength was reckoned at 80,000 horse, 200,000
foot, 8,000 chariots and 6,000 fighting elephants. There may
have been little exaggeration in this; twenty years later, the
great Indian conqueror Chandragupta – who as a young man

had seen Alexander – was in a position to give Seleukos 500 trained elephants, as the price of Seleukos' evacuation of the Punjab.

On the banks of the Beas that autumn, the army refused to go farther. The men gathered about the camp in groups talking gloomily, and falling silent if Alexander came near. Alexander called a conference of all officers. He wished, he said, to go on with a willing army, or not at all. He spoke much of glory – which shows how far out of touch with the inmost feelings of his men he now was. He said there was not much land left to conquer – 'one more river'; the Ganges led to the outer sea – and argued, as four years before in Iran, that to draw back with the work half done would invite rebellions, supported by the unconquered peoples. 'I hold,' he said, 'that for a brave man there is no end of labour except the labours themselves.' Finally he invited observations from any officer present.

There was a long silence. Then Koinos, than whom no king had an officer of more unquestioning loyalty, rose. He said that he wished to speak, not for the officers present, but for the men. His long and unquestioning service and the honours which the King had done him gave him the right to do so. He thought it was time to stop; all the more so, in view of the greatness of their achievements. The King knew how few were left of the original army that had left home eight years ago. Death in battle, discharge from wounds, sickness most of all, had taken their toll. The men were tired out, mentally even more than physically. They wanted to see their parents and wives and children and their home country, and to display and enjoy the wealth and position which they owed to the King. Even the Greeks left in the new cities were growing restive. Let the King go home in triumph after his great deeds, see his mother, re-organize Greece; and afterwards, if he wished, he could make another expedition with a fresh army, either to India, or to the Black Sea, or to Carthage and the west, with young men instead of these weary veterans. The officers applauded Koinos, many of them in tears. Alexander, in great displeasure, dismissed the meeting.

Next day he summoned them again and said that he was going on, but he wished to take no man who was unwilling. The rest could go home – and tell their families that they had deserted their King in the face of the enemy. He then shut himself up in his tent for three days, hoping for a revulsion of feeling. But the camp remained in gloomy silence, the men troubled that Alexander was angry, but showing no intention of changing their minds. At last he sent for the most senior Companions and told them he had decided to go back. The troops wept for joy, and crowded round the tent to cheer Alexander and call down blessings upon him.

Alexander would go home, but not back on his tracks. First he must subdue the lower Punjab, and he would also explore the lower Indus and the sea, of which he had now heard, from here back to the Persian Gulf. On the Beas he built twelve vast altars to the Twelve Gods, beginning with Zeus-Ammon, sacrificed, and held the usual athletic sports. Then returning to the Jhelum, he manned his river flotilla and, embarking on it the Hypaspistai, archers, Agriânes and Royal Squadron of the horse-guards, started downstream, Krateros with a corps following the right bank, by land, and Hêphaistion with the elephants and the main body the left.

But Koinos fell sick and died on the Jhelum, without seeing again the wife he had married just before leaving home. Alexander, his grudge forgotten, gave him a marshal's funeral.

Fighting in India was not over; the Malloi and Oxydrakai, the tribes on the lower course of the five rivers, a stubborn folk not ruled by kings, resisted Alexander fiercely. The result was yet another campaign of horrible carnage, worse, perhaps, than the conquering march down the Kabul valley; not so much, probably, because the troops were sick of fighting and wanted to make an end, as merely because the population was thicker on the ground. Neither Alexander nor his troops had lost any of their fearful efficiency. A fifty-mile short-cut across the desert, in an afternoon and a night, led to a dawn surprise and slaughter at the first city of the Malloi. Cavalry, unsupported by infantry, harassed and halted the retreat of a large force, until archers and spearmen came up and they could be broken and slaughtered. When 'combing' the river banks, Alexander sent a force under Hêphaistion five days ahead to kill fugitives, and left another under Ptolemy three days' march behind to catch any who broke back. A city of Brahmans was destroyed with almost all its 5,000 inhabitants, some of whom burnt their own houses over their heads; 'and few were taken alive, because of their courage'.

The adventure which befell at another citadel of the Malloi requires more notice from a biographer of Alexander, since it may have shortened his life. There had been some delay in bringing up scaling ladders. The lower town had fallen at the first rush, and Perdikkas' division had thought they would not be wanted. Only two were at hand, and the Macedonians were slow about planting them. Alexander impatiently seized one himself and, with his shield over his head, began to climb it. Behind him went Peukestas, who carried the sacred shield that Alexander had taken from Troy, and Leonnâtos the body-guard. Alexander reached the top, hooked his shield over the battlements, parried the blow of a Mallian who attacked him, killed the man, and was up, fighting furiously. He killed some and drove others over the wall inside, where the slope of the ground made the drop a short one. Peukestas and Leonnâtos followed, and, by the other ladder, Abreas, a corporal of the foot-guards. The guards, seeing the King in danger, swarmed up the ladders behind, overloaded them, and both ladders broke.

Alexander was left on the wall, a vivid figure in his gleaming armour and a target for every archer in the surrounding towers; though no one now dared to approach the space which he had cleared. Rather than wait to be picked off, he jumped down – *inside*. An Indian captain rushed at him, only to fall by his sword. He felled another with a great stone, and then a third; a fourth man got to close quarters and fell to his sword also. The three on the wall meanwhile leapt down to join him. Now the defenders no longer dared to approach, but held off, attacking only with every missile at their command. Abreas fell with an arrow through his face. Then Alexander was struck by a heavy arrow, clean through the breastplate into his lung. He still stood for a while, arterial blood and bubbles oozing round the shaft; then, dizzy and fainting, sank slowly down between his shield and the wall. Peukestas, bestriding him with the sacred shield of Ilion, and Leonnâtos on the other side, covered him as best they could and waited their turn.

Outside, the guards in frenzy flung themselves at the mud wall. Some drove in pegs and mounted on them. Some climbed on each other's shoulders. Superhuman feats of strength and agility were done; and now a few reached the top and sprang down where the King lay, cries of dismay mingling with the battle yell. They hacked open a tiny postern gate which let in one man at a time; and then, finding themselves in a narrow gateway, a group of them braced themselves across it and, with a frantic heave of their great shoulders, pushed a section of the mud wall bodily over! The whole brigade poured in, and massacred every man, woman and child whom they found in the citadel.

They carried Alexander out on his shield, between life and death. There was no doctor at hand, but they sawed off the shaft and got his breastplate off. The arrow-head had buried iself just above the nipple; a huge thing, four inches by three. Alexander said, 'Cut it out.' Perdikkas did so, with his sword; blood flowed, and Alexander fainted again. His doctor, Kritodêmos, of the great medical school of Kos, came and attended him, but for days it was uncertain whether he could live.

There was gloom and dismay in the camp. The troops might be exasperated at times with Alexander's insatiable lust for conquest, or with his Iranian dress and monarchy (this trouble had been little heard of since they left Iran); but he was still Alexander, the King who was like no one else, who had led them to wealth and power undreamed of, the ever-victorious, the generous giver, the leader who shared their every danger and hardship; they loved and admired him even when they were most angry with him; and now he was taking them home.

Also, there was no obvious second-in-command. Who handled the greatest business? Krateros? Hêphaistion? Perdikkas?

Ptolemy? Above all, no one had been *appointed* to take command if Alexander should die. Would the great marshals be able to agree, if the worst came to the worst? And could anyone but the King really get them home?

News came that Alexander was better, but few believed it. The army had developed a soldier's 'sales-resistance' to cheering official news. And then, as soon as he could move, Alexander had himself brought down by ship to the main camp at the confluence of the Jhelum and Sutlej. He had his awnings on deck removed, so that the men could see him; but even then they thought they were being shown the corpse of Alexander, till he waved to them. Then everyone cheered together, 'some stretching out their hands to heaven, and some toward Alexander'.

The guards had brought a palanquin down to the bank; but he called for a horse, was lifted on to it, and having ridden to his tent, let them see him walk into it. Joy passed all bounds, and men pressed round to touch him or to throw ribbons over him, or flowers (it was now spring of our year 325). His friends reproached him for so risking his life doing the work of a private soldier. At this Alexander showed a certain irritation: 'and I think' – says Arrian – 'that this was because he knew the criticism was just; and yet, for the warlike spirit and love of glory that was in him, as other men yield to other temptations, so he could not keep out of danger'.

The Malloi, who remained, submitted; and with relatively little fighting Alexander descended the Indus. He left Pôros as vassal-King of most of the Punjab; Philip, brother of Harpalos, as Governor of the Indus province; Oxyartes, the father of Roxâne, as Governor of Paropamisadai, the old Persian Satrapy west of Arachosia, and a certain Apollophanes of Gedrosia (Beluchistan), which an army under Leonnâtos was left to conquer.

Near Pattala, at the head of the Indus delta, he established a naval station. For himself, he had determined to sail that sea, as once to set foot beyond the Danube; and then to send a squadron of his larger ships, to follow the coast to the Euphrates' mouth, establishing the sea-route to his Indian Empire. The fleet was manned chiefly by Phœnicians, Cypriotes, Lykians and Egyptians (even now, there were few men from the Greek maritime republics). Its admiral was Nearchos the Cretan, Alexander's boyhood friend, who after governing Lykia for four years had rejoined with drafts in Bactria. Admiral and crews had had plenty of experience together, including experiences of gales and broken water, on the Indus and Jhelum.

The south-west monsoon was now blowing again, and the fleet would have to wait for autumn before adventuring on the open sea. Some damage to ships was also suffered from the unfamiliar ocean tides. Alexander, however, sailed out to an off-shore island and sacrificed bulls to Poseidon. Then he set off with his light troops (but with a long baggage train, including the troops' women and children) to follow the coast back to Persia, to explore it, make contact with the inhabitants, dig wells and establish food-dumps for the fleet when it should follow. Meanwhile Krateros, with the main body and the elephants, would follow the main route farther north through Gedrosia and Drangiana to Carmania in south-central Iran.

It was a hard route by which Alexander proposed to travel. Reports said that both Cyrus and the mythical conquering Queen Semiramis had extricated themselves from it with the almost total loss of their armies. But his self-confidence was unshaken.

For the first time in his life he had really overreached himself.

It was high summer, and the sun blazed pitilessly on the shifting sand-dunes, where the wagons stuck and the beasts – horses and mules, not camels – sank fetlock-deep 'as though struggling in soft snow'; and the necessity of taking a line that the waggons could follow increased the length of stages and threw out the timetable. The waterless coast of the Mekran proved so fearsome that they were compelled after all to take a route somewhat inland. A reconnoitring party, sent down to an inhabited point on the coast, returned with reports of a poverty-stricken fishing population, whose very beasts ate fish, and tasted of it; whose clothes were of fish-skins, their huts roofed with shells and their water a brackish liquid scooped from holes in the pebble beaches. The army was already going hungry, and the escort of a convoy actually ventured to break the royal seals on sacks of grain collected for the fleet, from the less arid inland regions, and to eat the contents. Alexander was constrained, after hearing their excuses, to forgive the crime. He collected more grain personally from the wretched inhabitants, and established depots at two points, commanding the natives also to collect more flour, ready ground, dates and sheep ready for slaughter; all these would be paid for.

This done, they marched on for Poura, the capital of Gedrosia. Difficulties did not diminish. Another 'sand sea' was encountered, and exhaustion and indiscipline increased day by day. As usual in summer, they marched by night; but the stages between water and water were often longer than could be completed in darkness, and ended with nightmare hours of fatigue and thirst, marching in the morning sun. Also, marching in the dark encouraged bad discipline. Many men fell out, and by no means all those who lay down in the night to sleep succeeded in rejoining on the following day. Mules and horses foundered from exhaustion and thirst; others were killed for food, and reported at the next halt as having foundered; while the wagons were broken up for firewood. Alexander knew what was going on, but felt it useless to punish, and pretended to believe the delinquents' stories. Presently there were not enough wagons to carry the sick, and those who could not keep up on foot were left behind. So far, however, few of the women and children had been lost.

Then came a crowning disaster.

One night they camped in a deep wadi, and far away in the mountains it rained; a torrential downpour, an outlying storm of the Indian monsoon. 'In the second watch of the night' – perhaps before many of the exhausted sleepers had woken – the camp was awash, and in a few moments more, the wadi was filled from bank to bank by a roaring torrent. Most of the men got out with their personal arms, and the cavalry with their horses – the discipline of years still held to that extent – but many were drowned; and, especially, the majority of the women and children were lost, and practically all the wagons and baggage animals that had carried them so far. Now at least there was unlimited water, and several of the survivors died from drinking too much.

In increasing misery the remainder staggered on. Water ran short again, and they missed the next water-hole. A party searching for it found a pool in a wadi, and brought some in a helmet to Alexander. 'We meant it for our children,' they said; 'but we can get more children if you survive!' Alexander thanked and praised the givers, but, looking round at the thirsty men behind him, refused to drink it. He was still the leader.

There was not a landmark to be seen, neither tree nor permanent hill; all previous tracks had been covered by the shifting sand, and at last the local guides, ignorant of the Greek and Phœnician science of navigating by the sun or stars, confessed that they were lost.

Only one geographical fact remained certain: that the sea was somewhere on the left. Alexander himself took a squadron of cavalry and went to look for it; but one after another their horses collapsed exhausted. Leaving them and most of the men behind, Alexander pushed on on foot with a small party. With his last five companions he reached the shore and, like the 'fish-eaters', they scrabbled for water among the stones of the beach. They found it, fresh and plentiful, and went back for the others. With this incentive, the survivors of the column staggered down to the sea.

Thence for seven days they followed the shore, finding water by digging. What food they had, if any, does not appear; probably they ate horse. Then the guides at last picked up a landmark. The worst was over, and they struck inland through less arid country; Alexander avoided camping too close to plentiful water-supplies to avert further deaths from over-drinking. Two months after leaving civilized country in India they reached Poura, where they rested, and then proceeded by easy stages on to Carmania.

Here Krateros came in with the main body and elephants; and here, too, the trusty Stasânor and Pharasmanes, son of Phrataphernes, having feared the worst as soon as they heard that Alexander was marching by the coast, met the army with droves of baggage animals, especially camels, for lack of which in the desert the whole expedition had so nearly perished.

12 The End of the Adventure
(Persia to Babylon, 325–3)

Alexander found mountains of administrative work awaiting him. Apollophanes in eastern Beluchistan was proving dilatory, and his dismissal involved two other transfers. Philip in India had been murdered in a mutiny of Greek troops, but his Macedonian guards had suppressed it. Alexander wrote to 'Taxiles' and the military commander Eudêmos to take over the province temporarily.

Far more serious, however, was the evidence of widespread misconduct and misrule. Many governors had not expected him to come back from India and – apart from acts of extortion and oppression – had hired excessive numbers of mercenaries, presumably to ensure their positions in the event of his death. Kleandros, son of Polemokrates, and the Thracian Sitalkes, who had been in command at Ecbatana since the execution of Parmenion, were accused by the Medes of tomb-robbing and rapacity and brutality. Alexander heard the evidence of some of their own troops and found the complaints confirmed; and, apparently to their great surprise – for they had come in voluntarily to report – they were arrested, tried and put to death. The exemplary punishment of these two senior officers had a most salutary effect on the feelings of the governed.

At Pasargadai the same fate befell one Orxines, who had commanded the Persian territorial division of Gaugamêla. On the death of the Satrap of Persia, he had taken over the province without orders, 'to keep it for Alexander'; his motives were dubious, and he, too, had put many men to death and looted tombs; he had even permitted or been concerned in the looting of the mausoleum of King Cyrus. In Media a certain Baryaxes had proclaimed himself King of the Medes and Persians; but Atropates – one of the best satraps – had captured him and sent him to Alexander. A little later, at Susa, the Satrap of Susiana was executed with his son; the latter, it is said, killed by Alexander with his own hand. His officials noticed with alarm the King's growing severity. Apart from these glaring cases, he punished minor delinquencies severely, too, on the principle that he that is unfaithful in a little is unfaithful also in much.

One high official did not come to report : Alexander's school-time friend, the Treasurer Harpalos. None of the great officials had been more arrogant than he. He had lived in regal magnificence at Babylon, since succeeding Mazaios, keeping a private army, paying divine honours to his late Athenian mistress, the courtesan Pythionîke, and requiring people to bow before her successor, Glykera, as before a queen. His accounts were in chaos, and rather than face Alexander he fled – if such a progress can be called flight; for he arrived in Greece with 6,000 mercenaries, 5,000 talents in gold, and thirty warships, put in at the little harbour below the holy place of Tainaron (Cape Matapan), and asked to be received at Athens, where he was *persona grata*, having provisioned the city during a recent famine. The Athenians, however, though still jealous of Alexander, declined to take a step that meant open war, and Harpalos, passing over to Crete, was ultimately murdered after some disturbance among his soldiers.

Hêphaistion was still quarrelling with Eumenes, and Alexander had to speak severely to him after a typically childish incident when his servants threw Eumenes' servants and baggage out of a billet which both officers wanted. Even in Macedonia there was trouble at court; Antipatros and Olympias kept writing furious letters about each other, the old general complaining of the Queen's interference in affairs, and she of the general's arrogance and assumption of power. 'She demands a heavy rent for nine months,' said Alexander wearily, after reading some of their correspondence.

Kassandros, son of Antipatros, came out to give explanations; but he was guilty of laughing when he saw Persians prostrating themselves, and Alexander, in a paroxysm of rage, seized him by the hair and beat his head against the wall. The episode did not help Antipatros ... Years afterwards Kassandros, a powerful character himself, is reported to have turned sick and faint at sight of a statue of Alexander.

However, there was good news as well as bad, and rewards to be administered as well as punishments. Nearchos arrived, lean, bearded and travel-stained, but safe, with his ships. They had left the Indus a month early because of the increasingly unfriendly attitude of the inhabitants, once the army had gone, and consequently had been becalmed for nearly a month before the easterly monsoon blew. They had suffered from thirst and from shortages of food; but they had met no formidable weather. Their chief adventure had been an encounter with a school of whales. The sight of the creatures 'spouting' first suggested to the sailors a discharge from man-made machines. When some Indians on board told them that this was done by sea-monsters, there was a panic, which Nearchos allayed by giving orders to man catapults, blow trumpets and charge, prepared to ram. The whales vanished hastily.

Nearchos afterwards wrote an account of his voyage, from which some information is preserved by Arrian.

At Susa, Alexander held an investiture. He had already enrolled Peukestas, who had saved his life among the Malloi, as an eighth or supernumerary bodyguard, so that he might enjoy this honour, the staff appointment closest to the King, before going to the governorship of Persia, for which he had already been designated. Alexander now decorated him with a crown of gold; then the body-guard Leonnâtos, for gallantry on the same occasion and for distinguished service on his independent command in Beluchistan; then Nearchos and his helmsman and navigator Onêsikritos (who also wrote a book, characterized according to Arrian by extreme mendacity); and then the other six bodyguards, Hêphaistion, Perdikkas, Ptolemy, Lysimachos, Peithon and Aristonoos.

Alexander also returned vigorously to his policy of trying to combine Macedonians, Medes and Persians into one 'master-race', and held, at Susa, the famous 'wedding of east and west', at which he married Stateira, daughter of Dareios, and caused eighty of his most distinguished officers to marry the daughters of distinguished Persians. Hêphaistion was given Drypetis, sister of Stateira, 'so that his children and Alexander's might be cousins'; Krateros, the daughter of Dareios' brother; Perdikkas, the daughter of Atropates of Media; Ptolemy and Eumenes, two daughters of Artabazos; Nearchos, a daughter of Artabazos' eldest daughter by her first husband, the Rhodian soldier Mentor (elder brother of Memnon). Seleukos, now commander of the Silver Shields, was given Apame, the daughter of a gallant enemy, Spitamenes, the hero of Sogdiana; he alone did not put away his Persian bride after Alexander's death, and several cities were named after her, Apameia. Shortly afterwards, Alexander added to his harem Parysatis, the youngest daughter of the former King Ochos, as one more link with legitimacy.

It is sometimes said that ten thousand such weddings of Macedonians to Persian women were celebrated simultaneously; but this is an exaggeration. What Alexander did do was to give handsome dowries to about 10,000 of his troops who had married Asiatic women already.

At the same time he gave the title of Companions to the Iranian cavalry regiments which had distinguished themselves in India, and he introduced the sons of Mazaios, of Artabazos, of Phratraphernes of Parthia, and of Oxyartes, the father of Roxâne, into the Royal Squadron.

Peukestas, as Governor of Persia, threw himself into this policy with vigour, learnt the language and adopted native dress in his province; but most of the Macedonians regarded it with deep gloom. Consciously, they feared to lose their privileged position, and resented seeing 'barbarians' placed on a level with them. It is easy enough for modern historians to blame them for not sharing the lofty *Weltanschauung* attributed to Alexander; but it is really unjust. They had not objected to seeing Paionians or Thracians rise high among Alexander's officers;

nor was there any 'colour-bar' against Asiatics as such (nor were Persians a different colour from Greeks). They had two good reasons for disliking Alexander's policy of fusion. First, the Iranians were accustomed to (and would support Alexander in) the Oriental absolute monarchy that he was establishing – a menace to the popular, accessible, in effect limited, Macedonian monarchy; and, second, the Iranians were so numerous. When they struggled in conscious, selfish defence of their privileged position, they were fighting, perhaps only half-consciously against absorption; for their national identity; for their freedom as they knew it – the cause for which both individuals and nations commonly resist to the uttermost and are not usually blamed.

Alexander also attempted to clarify his position vis-à-vis the Greek city-states. Antipatros, apart from being on bad terms with Olympias, was reported to be inclined to favour oligarchies in Greece, no doubt finding them less intractable than democracies. Alexander determined to replace him by Krateros, who would be charged with 'protecting the liberties of the Greeks', and to summon Antipatros to bring out the next large draft of Macedonian recruits. He must have been too old for much active campaigning (he was probably over seventy), but would probably have been used in a similar capacity as 'Minister of the Interior' in Asia during the next war of conquest, as he had already been in Macedonia.

Alexander's other two measures were more controversial. He sent orders to the Greek states to restore all exiles (which involved restitution of their property), and he apparently asked for the payment of divine honours to himself.

He probably regarded the former as a great act of appeasement, for most of the exiles were in exile simply for being anti-Macedonian; but he was obviously far exceeding any powers voted to him as Captain of the League, and the Synod of the League seems only to have been brought into the affair by being required to see to the circulation of the royal ukase. Feeling at Athens (as no doubt elsewhere) was at once up in

arms; the Athenians had also (again like other people) an ulterior motive for objecting, in that they had recently settled a
considerable number of citizens on the lands of the exiled
plutocracy at Samos, which had become in effect an Athenian
possession. The practical problems of reabsorption were going
to be difficult.

As regards the question of divine honours, it must always
be remembered that the view that many – some even said all –
of the Olympic gods had really been human beings was gaining
ground in Greece, especially in many 'rationalist' circles. The
request, if made, was not, therefore, particularly shocking to
Greek religious susceptibilities. There had already been cases in
the last hundred years of men of heroic attainments being
honoured as gods; a form of honour, be it remembered, that did
not demand belief in their omnipotence, or omniscience, or
sinlessness, or the immortality of their bodies, or any such
blatant absurdity. The Spartan Lysander at the height of his
power had been honoured in this way at Samos, and a pupil of
Isokrates, named Klearchos, as despot of Hêrakleia on the Black
Sea, had been 'worshipped' in this sense – which is far from the
Hebrew and Christian sense – by his subjects. Aristotle himself,
in a passage in his *Politics*, seems to countenance this idea of
the divinity of the 'godlike man'; and in the next generation
Athens, by acclamation, gave divine honours to Dêmêtrios, son
of Antigonos the One-Eyed. Lysander, Klearchos and Dêmêtrios
are a rather curious selection; no one had tried to worship
Agêsilaos or Epameinôndas, for example; which prompts the
question what the three had in common. It was probably the
combination of great achievements with a certain vividness of
person and personality – 'personal magnetism', in fact. Alexander was certainly well qualified under both heads.

No, what irritated many Greeks must have been, not the feeling that deification of a man was blasphemous or absurd, but
simply the nature of Alexander's approach to them. They were
sensitive of their position as free men; they would honour
Lysander or Klearchos or Dêmêtrios if they chose, but they
were not going to have their god-men imposed upon them.

Alexander's relations with Athens were extremely strained for a time, but, thanks to mutual concessions in the matter of the exiles, and to the city's refusal to assist Harpalos, the disaster for Athens of an open breach was avoided.

With the approach of spring (324) Alexander prepared to move to Ecbatana, the cooler, higher, Achaimenid summer capital, for the hot weather. There could be no great military expedition this year; first, he must reorganize the army, incorporating the young Asiatic soldiers trained in the last six years by Macedonian officers; but his brain was already busy with many projects. First – even before the long-projected Black Sea expedition – he would lead a seaborne expedition to the coasts of Arabia, opening up the sea routes from Egypt to India. Later – for his 'sphere of influence' already included Cyrenaica and touched the Adriatic – he might take in Carthage and the western Mediterranean. Meanwhile he sent out explorers down the Persian Gulf. In the spring he descended himself from Susa for a short voyage there, and then returned via the Tigris to Opis, near Babylon, to supervise the demobilization of the older Macedonian soldiers.

He reckoned that 13,000 foot and 2,000 horse – just the original paper strength of the Macedonian units that had crossed the Dardanelles ten years ago – would be a sufficient number of Macedonians to keep in his standing army. This would be inclusive of the new drafts which Antipatros was to bring out. Meanwhile the 30,000 Asiatic troops had been brought in by the satraps responsible for them – Peukestas among them, viewed askance by the Macedonians, in his Persian embroidered jacket and trousers – to a central camp. Atropates of Media even produced 100 horsewomen, alleged to be genuine Amazons; but Alexander decided that women in the army would be a source of more trouble than they were worth. That left about 10,000 Macedonians due for discharge, and at Opis Alexander informed them what classes he proposed to demobilize, with full pay during the journey home, and a handsome bonus.

Probably to his sincere surprise, the Macedonians received the speech with a roar of dissent. This, they felt, was the crisis. Thus far, for all the King's Orientalizing, the Macedonians were still the core of his army and he had to pay them some attention. After this, if he had his way, they would be a third of it. They attempted, not so much a mutiny as a strike. 'No!' they shouted: 'Let us *all* go, and fight your battles with your Persians and your father Ammon!'

The last taunt stung Alexander to the quick; he had never disowned Philip, especially in his dealings with the Macedonians, though both flatterers and mischief-makers had drawn that inference. He sprang down from the platform and went through the ranks with his guards, ordering, 'Arrest that man – and him – and him –' till he had pointed out thirteen men whom he had observed leading the shouting. All thirteen were executed that night, untried, on the King's order alone.

Then he returned, in dead silence, and delivered a scathing harangue. They might go, he said, when and where they liked; but first they should listen. Then, with great cunning, he assailed them for their ingratitude to *his father Philip*, who had 'found them nomadic mountain shepherds in skin coats, precariously defending their scanty flocks against Illyrians and Triballoi', and had made them masters of the peninsula. He went on to speak of his own achievements, from which they were the gainers. Had any man of them been wounded oftener than he had? Had he gained anything that he had not shared with them? Was there any material difference between them 'except this purple cloak and the ribbon round my brow? I eat as you eat, and sleep as you sleep; or, rather, I do not eat so richly as the more luxurious livers among you; and I rise early to plan that you may sleep soundly.'

His last word was 'Go!' and with that he again leapt down from the platform and shut himself up in his quarters, where he remained invisible all that day and the next. On the third, he sent for the chief Persians and appointed them to commands in the new army (organized as an exact replica of the Macedonian) and to other official positions. The highest rank at court was to be that of the Royal Kindred, who were alone permitted, in the Persian manner, to kiss His Majesty.

The Macedonians were left in dumb consternation. Most of them had not the least desire for their *congé*, and Alexander had called their bluff. Finally the news of the creation of Persian Companies, Persian 'Silver Shields' and the like, touching their inmost regimental pride, broke them completely. A penitent crowd assembled before the royal quarters, throwing down their arms in surrender, offering to hand over the ringleaders, threatening not to leave, day or night, till Alexander should take pity on them. At last Alexander came out, and there was an affecting scene.

'And what hurt our feelings most of all,' concluded the men's spokesman, a grey-haired squadron-commander of the Companions, 'is that you have made Persians your kinsmen, and they can kiss you, and that has never happened to a Macedonian!'

'But I count you *all* my kinsmen,' said Alexander, smiling, 'and anyone who wishes may kiss me now!'

Many did, beginning with the grey-haired captain.

After that Alexander held an immense feast of reconciliation, attended by some 9,000 Macedonians and Iranians. The solemn libations were poured, with prayers by Greek priests and Persian Magi, 'that the two nations might *rule together*[1] in unity and concord', and all drank together; but those who sat nearest the King were Macedonians. A few days later the veterans set off home with their pay and bonuses of a whole talent per man; they were led by Krateros, with the phalanx-colonel Polyperchon as second-in-command, in case Krateros, who was in poor health, should be compelled to rest.

At Ecbatana that summer, during one of Alexander's great athletic, dramatic and musical festivals, Hêphaistion died, of a fever which he had refused to take seriously. Seven days before he had been in perfect health.

1. This phrase makes it quite clear that Alexander did not cherish any advanced views of the brotherhood of all mankind, as is sometimes maintained. His project was that of a joint *Herrenvolk*.

To the unprejudiced reader this gallant but conventional young officer, Alexander's chief 'yes-man', does not appear a specially admirable character; but to Alexander he was the one person who really understood, the chief sharer of his lonely eminence, and he mourned 'like Achilles for Patroklos'. Hêphaistion's Regiment of the Companions, it was decreed, should bear his name and receive the daily password as from him, 'for ever'. The great festival became his funeral games, in which no less than 3,000 athletes and artists took part; and official mourning lasted for a long time – perhaps until a mission, sent to consult the Oracle of Ammon, returned with the desired response that Hêphaistion should be worshipped as a hero. Stories were told that Alexander indulged in wilder orgies of grief – for example, that he had the doctor, whose instructions Hêphaistion had flagrantly disobeyed, impaled; but these Arrian, after carefully examining the evidence, expressly disbelieves.

Presently, however, work went on. Alexander ordered further exploration for the coasts of Arabia, the construction of a vast harbour for sea-going galleys at Babylon, and the building of ships on the Caspian to explore that sea too, less for military reasons than because Alexander 'wanted to know'.

He was also devising a revolutionary tactical reform of his infantry. In each file of the phalanx (sixteen deep) henceforth only four should be Macedonians, the file-leader, his second and third, and the rear-rank man, all 'extra-pay' men: as it were, a corporal and three leading-soldiers or lance-corporals. They alone would carry the sarissa; after all, three spear-points protruding in front of the front rank should be enough; and the other twelve would be Asiatics armed with bows or javelins and the short sword. Presumably a new battle-drill was to have been worked out whereby the archers would open the battle; then the men with heavy javelins would pass through them; and finally the whole mass would close, with the spearmen in front. Considerable precision of drill would be required to execute the passing-through movements.

Such a phalanx would have borne a remarkable resemblance

to the Roman legion of the middle Republic, in which the battle was opened by the troops armed with sword and javelin, and taken up if necessary by the *triarii* (or in an earlier phase, the *hastati*) armed with long spears. The phalanx, so far, it is interesting to see, in spite of all Philip's improvements, had shown at Issos and Gaugamêla just that fault through which it ultimately succumbed to the Roman legions: the same rigidity, and consequent tendency, if the front were stretched or bent, to break in two, leaving gaps, of which, but for his own faint-heartedness, Dareios might have taken more deadly advantage.

This reform, however, was probably still in embryo, when in late autumn Alexander set out – largely no doubt to 'blood' and practise the young Asiatic troops – on his last campaign, to tame the Kassite mountaineers, neighbours of the Ouxians, whose ancestors had once captured Babylon and maintained a barbaric empire there for centuries. The Kassites had often evaded Persian punitive expeditions by taking to their then forested hills and emerging again afterwards; but Alexander's winter campaigning prevented that. Two columns, under Alexander and Ptolemy, swept the whole country and solved the Kassite problem in a typical, bloody, Alexandrian campaign. Thence Alexander descended to Babylon again, to prepare the Arabian expedition and to transact other business.

He declined to be put off by the representation of the Chaldæans that the omens were unfavourable for his visit. This great ecclesiastical corporation had done nothing about the promised rebuilding of the temple of Marduk, because, as Alexander shrewdly suspected, they found it profitable, in the absence of any temple and temple expenses, to have the whole of their vast revenues (chiefly from land) available for salaries and perquisites.

With Alexander in Babylon, work started in earnest, with both army and local labour. Meanwhile Alexander received ambassadors from every part of the Western world, come officially to congratulate him on his safe return from the East – and incidentally to proffer divers requests and to pick up such information as they could about his intentions. Ambassadors had come from every city of the League of Corinth to present their Captain-General with golden wreaths – traditionally the highest honour paid by a Greek state. It was noted, moreover, that they came garlanded, as though to salute a god. Others had come from the Libyan tribes bordering on Cyrenaica; from the Bruttians and Lucanians of south Italy, where Alexander of Epeiros had fallen after many successes; from Etruria, from Carthage, even from tribes of Kelts and Iberians in the farthest west. One may hazard the guess that these latter missions may have been organized by Carthage, which might feel herself likely to be the next victim; it would be only common sense from Alexander's point of view to unify the Mediterranean basin, joining the more thinly populated western shores to the eastern, which he already controlled. His papers were found after his death, it is said, to contain notes for the construction of a vast navy in the Levant and for a road along the north coast of Africa; one may compare the 'Royal Roads' of Persia. Carthage, through her Phœnician connections, had successfully 'planted' her intelligence agents, and might have tried to organize the West; but her defeats in the next few years by Agathokles, the tyrant of Syracuse, show that she would have been in no position to resist Alexander.

No envoys came, to the best of Arrian's belief, from central Italy, where an obscure and long-drawn struggle of mountain sieges and surprises was in progress between the Samnite mountain confederacy and the plain-dwellers of Latium and Campania, organized by the growing market-city of Rome.

The hot weather had returned in Babylon before all was done, but by the 18th of the month Daisios (the 3rd of June, 323) the day was fixed for the departure of the Arabian expedition. There was an old Macedonian taboo on starting a campaign during Daisios, probably because at home all hands were then needed for the harvest. At the Granikos Alexander had got round it by ordering the keepers of the calendar to intercalate a second Artemisios, the previous month. Intercalation was a familiar idea, being frequentiy necessary with the old imperfect calendars, to keep the 'moons' in step with the solar year; but the Emperor of the East was emancipated from such necessities. Nobody was at all alarmed when, in Eumenes' office, the keeper of the official Journal recorded that the King (who had been late the night before at a party given by one Mêdios, now his chief social companion) had transferred his quarters to a garden-house across the river, and there slept beside the swimming-pool for coolness because he had a fever. He let the orders stand, for the fleet to sail on the 22nd, and for those troops who were to march down to the sea to start on the 21st.

Next day, after taking his bath, he went to his bed-chamber and rested, playing dice and talking with Mêdios. In the evening he bathed again, performed the daily sacrifice, and took a light supper; he was feverish during the night. On the 20th, after bathing and sacrificing, he lay in the bathing-room, talking with Nearchos and others about the Persian Gulf. He still spoke of starting on the 22nd. On the 21st and 22nd, however, he was worse, with high fever in the evening and at night; but on the 23rd he again felt better and, with his bed laid for coolness beside the swimming-pool, received his chief officers to discuss appointments. On the 24th he was in a high fever all day, but still performed the daily sacrifice, though he had to be carried out to the altar to do it; and he ordered his generals and chief officers to remain at hand, apparently simply from a sick man's fretful anxiety to have them near him. Then, wearying of where he was, he had himself taken back to the palace across the river, and got a little sleep, but the fever did not break. The generals and colonels came to his bedside; he knew them, but could not speak; and so he remained, apparently delirious at times, on the 25th and 26th.

The rumour had spread by now that he was already dead, and a crowd of Macedonians besieged the doors of the palace, demanding to see him, if alive, if only to say good-bye. They got their way at last by persistence, and filed silently past the bed. Alexander could not speak, but moved his head and hand a little, to show that he knew them.

That night Peukestas, Peithon and others slept in a neighbouring temple, in the hope of some revelation in a dream as to how to treat the sickness; but none came, and next day Seleukos and Menidas and Kleomenes, the finance officer for Egypt, asked of the god directly, whether they should bring the King to the temple; the answer given was that he was better where he was.

On the 28th, towards evening, at the age of thirty-two years and eight months, Alexander died.

13 The Heritage of Alexander

1. The Division of the Empire

'Alexander dead?' said Dêmades at Athens. 'Impossible! The whole world would stink!' Yet it was even so; and now men must accustom themselves to the fact that had so many times been prematurely reported.

Lord Salisbury once said that the head office of his party, when he was to form a government, reminded him of nothing so much as feeding-time at the zoo. It was much the same at Babylon in 323 – and the carnivora were loose. A dozen strong and ruthless generals watched each other narrowly, wondering how much power they could win – or whether, by way of a regency, one might win all. One man only set himself a limited objective from the first: the deep-eyed, hook-nosed Ptolemy secured the Satrapy of Egypt, and worked steadily to rule it as an independent power.

Roxâne's child – a boy – was born after a few weeks, and the Macedonian gentry (the officers and cavalry) agreed that he should reign as King Alexander; but the commons – the phalangite infantry – objected to the prospect of a long regency and found a spokesman in the long-unpromoted colonel, Meleagros. Their ideal was probably a reversion to the 'good old' Macedonian constitution of the days of King Philip. They proposed Alexander's half-brother Arrhidaios, perhaps not realizing the extent of his incapacity. Ultimately, as King Alexander and King Philip, it was agreed that the two princes should reign jointly, with a regency-council of Perdikkas, Leonnâtos, Antipatros and Krateros.

Seleukos remained commander of the footguards. Peithon secured for himself the vital command at Ecbatana, and

Lysimachos that in Thrace, controlling the Dardanelles. Antipatros, contrary to Alexander's last intention, was left in Macedonia, and most of the eastern satraps – Peukestas, Stasânor, Atropates, Phrataphernes and the others – in their existing commands. So also was Antigonos the One-Eyed in Phrygia, where he had already secured, by good government, strong local support. Eumenes, the only Greek among the chieftains, was maliciously given Cappadocia and the region north of it, which were still unsubdued. Leonnâtos was deputed to install him, but instead went on to Macedonia – where, indeed, Antipatros, faced by a Greek War of Independence, needed him badly. Perdikkas then installed Eumenes himself. These two alone of the great marshals really attempted to maintain a strong central power, Perdikkas because, as the Regent in *de facto* control of the Kings' persons, that power was his; Eumenes because, as a non-Macedonian, he had no support but legitimacy, and also from a typically Greek personal loyalty to the house that had made him.

During this manoeuvring, violent deaths began – in the women's apartments. Roxâne – alas! no more innocent than the conquistadores around her – lured her rival Stateira to her by a forged letter, had her (and her sister) murdered, and hid the bodies in a well. Dareios' mother, feeling that in Alexander she had lost her last friend, had already committed suicide. Shortly afterwards, Perdikkas succeeded in making away with Meleagros as an alleged mutineer.

Meanwhile the Empire remained remarkably quiet – a tribute to Alexander's work; but, naturally, no more was heard of his union of the races. Only in the Far East and West was there trouble – among the Greeks. Thirty thousand colonists in Bactria and the neighbouring lands, homesick for the blue Mediterranean, started to march home. Peithon met them with his Iranian cavalry and, demonstrating that he could starve them if he chose, herded them forlornly back. In Greece Antipatros and Leonnâtos were defeated by an allied army under the Athenian Leosthenes, Leonnâtos was killed and Antipatros shut up in Lamia; but Krateros came to the rescue; the revolt was checked at Krannon in Thessaly; and meanwhile the Athenian navy, and with it the democracy, as a force in world affairs, succumbed in two sea-fights, in the Dardanelles and off Amorgos, against the superior numbers of the Macedonian and Levantine fleets (322). Demosthenes was one of those hunted down thereafter by Antipatros' agents, and escaped capture by taking poison.

In 321 warfare between the Successors started in earnest, when Antipatros, Krateros, Antigonos and Ptolemy combined against Perdikkas, who had hoped to transfer his government to Macedonia, with the support of Olympias, and to strengthen his position by marrying Alexander's sister. Krateros, crossing to Asia Minor, was defeated by Eumenes and mortally wounded; but Perdikkas, trying to dispose of Ptolemy, was brought to a halt at the eastern edge of the Delta, where his troops, subverted by Ptolemy's propaganda, murdered him.

A new conference of the powers at Triparadeisos in Syria now confirmed the aged Antipatros as sole Regent, increased the power of Antigonos at the expense of Eumenes, and condemned the latter to death – but he was still at large with an army. Antipatros brought home the helpless Kings to Macedonia; but he died in 319, nominating as Regent not his son Kassandros, but Polyperchon, who had come home with Krateros and the veterans in 323. Kassandros thereupon rebelled, supported by Antigonos. Eumenes, supporting Polyperchon, as the legitimate power, tried to recover Asia by marching to join the eastern satraps, in arms against the over-mighty Peithon; but after some remarkable adventures and successes, he was captured in Iran by Antigonos and put to death (316). Antigonos had also driven Seleukos from Babylon and Peukestas from Persia; his power now extended from the Ægean to Iran, and Polyperchon, driven from Macedonia by Kassandros, fled to him for refuge.

During the regency of Antipatros, Queen Olympias had retired to Epeiros. She now returned with an army, in support of her grandson against the alleged usurpation of Philip Arrhidaios, while Kassandros, who had used her claims in support of his rebellion, was absent in Greece. Arrhidaios' troops refused to fight against the mother of the great Alexander, and she seized the opportunity to put him to death (317). She was already, in Antipatros' time, circulating (and no doubt believing) a preposterous story, of which nothing had been heard earlier, that Alexander had been murdered by Antipatros, with a poison conveyed to Babylon by Kassandros and administered by Kassandros' brother, the cup-bearer Iollas, having been brewed (in revenge for his nephew Kallisthenes) by Aristotle! During her brief space of power she put to death so many people that Kassandros on his return was able to procure her condemnation by a no doubt packed assembly of 'the Macedonian people', and killed her in turn. He then, to improve his personal position, married another daughter of Philip, Thessaloníke, and renamed after her his capital, the port of Therma, which still bears her name (Salonica).

The next phase was a struggle by Kassandros, Lysimachos, Ptolemy and Seleukos against Antigonos, who declined to surrender the provinces which he had taken by force, and accused Kassandros (truly) of keeping Roxâne and the child King Alexander as prisoners. The result was that Kassandros finally made away with them (310). Antigonos and Polyperchon then produced an alleged natural son of Alexander by a daughter of Artabazos; but Polyperchon, changing sides, made away with him the following year. The line of Alexander was extinct; whereupon Antigonos assumed the title of King, and his four rivals answered him by doing the same (about 306 B.C.).

Antigonos dominated nearer Asia for a time, but he never succeeded in entering Europe or Egypt, though his brilliant son Dêmêtrios gained a strong footing in Greece; he restored democracy at Athens and received divine honours there. But meanwhile Seleukos (who had been a refugee with Ptolemy), after Ptolemy had defeated Dêmêtrios before Gaza, had ridden from the field of victory with 500 horse to recover the East. While Antigonos was engaged in the West, he united the eastern provinces, ceded those in India to the great Indian conqueror Chandragupta for 500 trained elephants, and returned to join hands with Lysimachos in Asia Minor, and to overwhelm Antigonos at Ipsos in 301.

Lysimachos and Seleukos divided the spoils, with their frontier at the Taurus; but the homeland of Macedonia had still twenty-five years of intermittent agony before it. Dêmêtrios was still at large in Greece, and in 294 he killed the son and successor of Kassandros and seized Macedonia; but he was turned out in 288 by Lysimachos with the help of the young King Pyrrhos of Epeiros, grandson of Olympias' brother Arybas – the same Pyrrhos who then fared west to cross swords, brilliantly but with insufficient weight behind him, with the rising power of Rome. Dêmêtrios ended his life an honoured prisoner of Seleukos, who in 281 crowned his career of conquest by defeating and killing Lysimachos at Koroupedion; but in the moment of victory he was murdered by one Ptolemy Keraunos – 'the Thunderbolt' – the eldest son of the first Ptolemy, and brother of the reigning Ptolemy II – an exile to whom he had given protection. Keraunos was the next adventurer to seize power in Macedonia; but in 279 he was killed by a horde of Gauls, who raided far into Greece, and three years of sheer anarchy followed. It was then that the son of Dêmêtrios, Antigonos Gonatas, brave, patient and intelligent, who had maintained a precarious footing in Greece, came to the rescue, routed the Gauls in 276 and founded the dynasty in Macedonia which lasted till the Roman Conquest in 168.

2. The Succession States

Macedonia under the Antigonid dynasty was a modest, stable, national state, which played a useful part in history as the northern shield, against the outer barbarians, of a Greece which had by no means shot her bolt as a home of political experiments and philosophic thought; yet she seldom got a good 'press' from the historians either of Greece, where deep suspicions of Macedonian imperialism persisted, or of Rome, anxious to justify Roman aggression against her. The Macedonians, moreover, deemed it necessary for their 'security' to hold certain strategic points in Greece: Dêmêtrias (near modern Volo), Chalkis and Corinth; and their tenure of these 'fetters of Greece' naturally only increased Greek hostility.

In Greece proper the two strongest powers were now the federal Leagues of Aitolia and of Achaia, which came to include much of Arcadia, and gained its greatest success when the young general Arâtos captured the fortress of Corinth by a night surprise. These two states covered the mountain regions which, as we have seen (p. 36), remained the most fertile breeding-ground of Greek soldiers, now that the citizen population of the older cities was in decline, while their form of government is by no means the least interesting among the political experiments which we owe to Greece. But after Philip and Alexander no Greek state was ever completely a free agent. The Greek republics were overshadowed by the great new kingdoms; even when they strove to make head against the Antigonids they were usually constrained to lean for support – especially financial support – upon the Ptolemies of Egypt; these for their part were anxious not to be excluded from Greece and the Asia Minor coasts, their essential source of timber for the fleet and of mercenary soldiers. There is this much shadow of justification for the school historians, who commonly ignore the efforts of post-Alexandrian Greece, gallant and even enlightened as they often were.

Even Athens and Sparta, though 'effete' in the literal sense of the word, as shown by the declining strength of their citizen armies, had by no means said their last word in history. At Sparta, where the 'national socialist' class-state had degenerated into an oligarchy of a few score wealthy and much-intermarried families, two young Kings, Agis IV and Kleomenes III, attempted in an idealist spirit to restore the communist commonwealth, which they believed the old Sparta to have been. Their attempt was foredoomed. Agis (244–1), who declined to use force against his fellow-citizens, died on the scaffold, the victim of a conspiracy of the rich, whose position he threatened. Kleomenes, a fine soldier, carried through the reform by force, redistributed the land, liberated helots, and for a space controlled most of the Peloponnese with a Spartan army 20,000 strong; only to go down before an unholy alliance of the 'bourgeois' Achaian League and Macedonia, on the field of Sellasia in 222; to drag out his days in Egypt till 219, kept as a diplomatic pawn by a degenerate Ptolemy; and then to perish in an entirely unrealistic attempt to rouse the Greek people of rich and parasitic Alexandria against their monarch. He was followed (after 207) by a leader named Nabis, a violent, forcible and cruel revolutionary, under whom the Spartans actually beat off the assault of the Roman consul Flamininus, who had defeated Macedonia; but the time had passed by now for free Greek social experiments. Nabis had to make terms with Rome, and later, after he had been murdered by some Aitolians, the Spartan commune was suppressed with great brutality by the Achaian general Philopoimên.

Athens, crushingly defeated at sea in 322, was never again a serious military or naval power; but this was not through any decline in the courage of her young men, as was shown in the 'Chrêmonidean War' (267–2), when they stood a terrible siege in the attempt to get rid of the Macedonians with help (illusory as usual) from Egypt. But Athens was now turning into what she was under the Roman Empire, the chief 'university town' of the Hellenistic world. To her came the learned and learners from every side. She had still, in the days of Antigonos Gonatas, her philosophers, such as Epicurus (Epikouros), who combined a materialist metaphysic with a gentle ethic of friendship and doing no harm; still her dramatists, the most famous of whom was Menander (Menandros), though all that now produced was a polished comedy of manners, with such familiar stock characters as the brainless but well-meaning young man-about-town, the resourceful man-servant and the peppery but good-hearted uncle; among them, too, figures the 'line-shooting' boastful soldier, a stock character more intelligible when one realizes that this is a sketch of the men who had marched under Seleukos or Alexander.

But most influential of the movements that took root at Athens in the new age was one which owed its vigour chiefly to men from the Hellenized Levant – the very environment which, three centuries later, produced St Paul. This was the stoic philosophy, the philosophy of duty, fundamentally mono-theistic, the creation of a Hellenized Semite of Cyprus: Zênon, (c. 340–264) the gaunt, retiring thinker, come to Athens in search of wisdom, who taught in the public colonnades (Stoai) because, unlike Epikouros, he had not a private garden of his own; and who without money or influence or even attractive-ness as a teacher – he was actually too shy to give formal lec-tures – by sheer moral earnestness became a force in the world. One of his most intimate friends was none other than Antigonos Gonatas: the first Stoic King. After him his philosophy was car-ried on very largely by other Easterners: Kleanthes (c. 300–220), a Greek from Asia Minor, Chrysippos (c. 280–207), from Cilicia; Diogenes of Babylon, Antipatros from St Paul's own city of Tarsus. A pupil of these last two was Panaitios, of Rhodes, who influenced the great Roman Scipio Æmilianus (son of Æmilius, the conqueror of Macedon); and his pupil Poseidonios, from Apameia in Syria, influenced Pompey and Cicero. Stoicism came into its own, indeed, more than ever in the Roman world, in which it became in effect the religion of many statesmen and soldiers; among others, the Emperor Marcus Aurelius, who revered as among the greatest teachers a Stoic of the previous century, Epiktêtos the Phrygian slave.

In an age in which republicanism was fading, Stoicism did a great work in promoting a high ideal of kingship; no move-ment was either a more important or a more characteristic growth of the new cosmopolitan world created by the con-quests of Alexander.

Among the kingdoms sprung from the sundered Empire, that of the Ptolemies in Egypt lasted with great stability, if on the whole with diminishing vigour in the royal house, until the death of the last (the famous) Cleopatra in 30 B.C. It was a purely Greco-Macedonian monarchy – Cleopatra herself was probably the only ruler of her line who ever learned the native language – its capital the city-state of Alexandria, its pride the 'Museum', a state academy of Greek science and letters, with a magnificent library; organizing agriculture and taxing the un-regarded *fellahin* through an immense bureaucracy which was taken over as a revenue-producing machine by the Roman emperors.

The Empire inherited by Antiochos, the son of Seleukos, on the other hand – the trunk of the Empire, extending at first from the Ægean to India – was slowly but steadily breaking up throughout its career of some two hundred years, and its fate suggests what *might* well have happened, if on a larger and slower scale, even if Alexander had lived long enough to extend his conquests farther and to found a dynasty.

It was not for lack of vigorous kings at the top. The two great weaknesses were that, for all the Seleukids could do by founding yet more Greek cities and encouraging immigration, *there were not enough Greeks and Macedonians* to hold this vast expanse; and that, as the Empire was a new creation, and not based, like the Persian, on a race – except the Greco-Macedonian, whose homeland was outside its frontiers – there was no tradition of loyalty to check rebellions either at the centre or in remote provinces.

Internally the Seleukid Empire was based on a Macedonian army – though recruiting Greeks also, and making a certain limited use of Iranian contingents – and on its numerous Greek cities, which the dynasty founded as garrisons, centres of gov-ernment and nurseries of manpower. To think of them as 'foci of Greek culture' in the sense of deliberate missionary enter-prises for the benefit of the benighted natives is anachronistic, though they did, in fact, have that effect. The cities enjoyed complete local self-government as city-states, and in normal times were not even taxed, though in the continual crises they were often 'requested to contribute', with the practical force of a command.

The court was Macedonian, with a certain Oriental magnifi-cence, but with none of Alexander's Oriental ceremonies. The King, though he sometimes received divine honours even in his lifetime (especially from the Greek cities), and though his ances-tors were always deified, hunted and drank deep with his

Kindred, Chief Body-guards and Friends (all these were recognized ranks at court) and on occasion 'unbent' to an extent which serious Greeks found shocking, dancing or taking part in practical jokes. Alexander's ill-fated claim for prostration, at least by Greeks and Macedonians, had gone for ever.

Gone, too, was the great scheme for a union of the two 'master-races'; but in spite of the Macedonian reaction, Iranians sometimes, if rarely, rose to be generals or satraps even in the west – probably more often in Iran, where evidence is lacking. As more Greek men than women must have come east (especially soldiers), there was also no doubt a rapid dilution of blood. Was not the royal house descended from Spitamenes?

Had Alexander lived long enough to succeed in imposing his policy of uniting Macedonians, Greeks and Iranians, one might perhaps have seen the Empire show more durability; but under his successors it must surely also have become rapidly Orientalized, unless the policy had then, after all, been reversed. As it was, though the mixture of blood took place all the same, the culture of the Empire remained purely Greek. At the very end, in the disastrous last century B.C., the poems of such Syrian Greeks as Antipatros of Sidon and Meleagros of Gadara (collector of the first *Greek Anthology*) are pure Greek elegiacs – but with a luscious and sensuous beauty, especially in Meleagros, which is not so much like any literature of the older Greece as like the *Song of Songs*.

Externally, the Empire was crumbling from the first. Seleukos the Conqueror himself had shed the Indian provinces. The north-east of Asia Minor was never conquered, and here sprang up the native kingdoms of Bithynia (under kings with Greek names) and of Pontos, Cappadocia and Armenia, all under Iranian dynasties. The Gauls broke into western Asia Minor – ferried across, during the chaos after the deaths of Seleukos and Keraunos, on shipping provided by the local Greek cities, anxious only to get rid of them; they founded Galatia, keeping their Keltic language but adding local cults to their religion. Their raids into Greek Ionia were ultimately curbed by a new kingdom based on the fortress of Pergamon, where a Greek

eunuch named Philetairos, placed there in charge of Lysimachos' gold reserve, made himself independent. His nephew
Eumenes (reigned 263–241) and his successors (called alternately Eumenes and Attalos) defeated both Gauls and Seleukids, commemorated their victories in famous though florid
sculpture and kept a library second only to that of Alexandria.
Meanwhile the Seleukids kept open a corridor to the Ægean, no
doubt commercially important, along the north side of the
southern mountains, until Roman intervention drove Antiochos
III beyond the Taurus in 190 B.C.

In Iran, disruption began about 250, when Diodotos, the
Greek Satrap of Bactria, proclaimed himself independent during
Antiochos II's wars with Ptolemy II, the Gauls and Pergamos.
The new kingdom displayed great vigour; evidently it had, like
Pergamos, the full support of the people – especially the colonists, here Greek rather than Macedonian – whom the harassed
central government had left to their own resources. But while
Diodotos was engaged in conquering Sogdiana, the historic frontier between Iran and Turan was left open farther west, and a
tribe of Iranian-speaking nomads under a chief named Arsakes
broke into Parthia, which had not been so intensively colonized
as the frontier region, killed the Satrap (who was also thinking
of making himself independent) and established themselves as
the aristocracy of a new Parthian kingdom (c. 248).

Parthia was small and weak at first, afraid of Diodotos of
Bactria and quite unable to make head against the Seleukids
when they had their hands free; but the wars of the succession-
states let it take root. Its kings acquired at least a veneer of
Greek culture; in its later days some of them bore the surname, 'The Phil-Hellene' (as against Rome?) and Greek plays
were performed at Court. When the Seleukid Empire was being
weakened by Rome (encouraging, for example, the Jewish
rebellion under the Maccabees against the Hellenizer Antiochos
IV Epiphanes, 175–164, and his successors), Parthia was the
chief gainer, winning Media about 150 and Babylonia about 140.
Persia seems to have revived as a dependent kingdom, nursing in its mountains the pure form of the Zoroastrian religion

and the memory of a golden past; one day to burst upon the world again with the Sassanid Empire.

The Macedonians of Syria fought stoutly to recover Babylonia, but had lost it finally by 129. Indeed, throughout their career, the Seleukid kings repeatedly marched east and, like the later Roman emperors, were rarely beaten in the field; but rebellions, other frontiers, and insufficient manpower never let them consolidate. By 88 B.C. the Parthians were on the Upper Euphrates. Even Syria was now breaking up into its component cities. The *coup de grâce* was given by an ephemeral Armenian conquest, after which Pompey, in 64, made Syria a Roman province.

The Hellenism of Bactria ultimately perished from the same cause: lack of firm roots – i.e. lack of manpower (and, perhaps still more, of Greek womanpower), and lack of loyalty to the parvenu monarchy; but it developed for a time an aggressive power and an artistic activity that speaks volumes for the strength of the colonies planted here by Alexander and reinforced by Seleukos and the first Antiochos. When Antiochos III (the Great) marched east, the last Seleukid to reach the Oxus, the kingdom probably included the old Satrapies of Arachosia, Drangiana, part of Areia, Bactriana and Sogdiana; with the cities that are now Herat, Kandahar, Balkh, Bokhara, Samarkand and Khodjend. King Euthydêmos induced Antiochos to be content with a very nominal suzerainty, by pointing out to him how war between Greeks here could have no other effect than to let in the jungle, in the shape of the nomad hordes of Turan; but when Antiochos had been rendered 'harmless' by Rome (190), he so far forgot his defensive functions as to plunge into a war of conquest in India. His son Dêmêtrios reached the mouth of the Indus; but Nemesis followed, when one Eukratids, perhaps a Seleukid general, seized Bactria behind him. He then made himself king; so there were two kingdoms, north and south of the Hindu Kush, and soon pretenders to the throne, most of them known only by their coins, arose on every side. As a result, the Parthians captured Herat, and Mongolian tribes, the Yueh-Chi, according to Chinese sources, overran Sogdiana about 160 and Bactria about 140 B.C. When the Chinese general Pan Chao crossed Turkestan about A.D. 97,[1] he found only barbarism.

The Greco-Indian kingdom lasted longer, perhaps till about 40 B.C., but it was growing steadily less Greek. Its coins are artistically degenerate, as compared with the magnificent issues of the earlier kings, with vivid portrait heads (Eukratides, by the way, wears a sun-helmet) and such 'reverse' types as the Indian elephant and the Greek horsemen of Bactria. After Eukratides and Dêmêtrios, native legends appear on the coins. Meanwhile Greek sculpture in stone also entered the East, and Gandara in Afghanistan later became the cradle of Buddhist sculpture, under a profound Greek influence.

As a parallel in literature we have the Milinda Dialogues. In this work of Buddhist popular philosophy, of perhaps the second century A.D., the historical Greek King Menandros – 'king of the viciously valiant Ionians' to the Indian writer – whose long reign may have been about 120 to 80 B.C., who is known to us only from his coins, with the surname of 'The Just', and from a mention by the geographer Strabo as having pushed farther east than Alexander, appears as an earnest seeker after truth, putting his questions to and finally convinced by the Buddhist sage Nagasena: Europe giving way at last to India on Indian soil.

1. I decline to be intimidated by the pedants who forbid us to use this convenient abbreviation, on the ground that A.D. can only stand for *anno Domini*. It can just as well stand for *annorum* D., if anyone wants to apply Latin grammar to an English idiom.

Nearer the Mediterranean, in the Near or, as our generation has come to call it, the Middle East ('Middle' in the sense
of being intermediate between Europe and the remoter east,
from India to China), Hellenistic culture long outlasted the
absorption of the Hellenistic states by Rome. This Greek culture – Greek at least in that this was the language of nearly
all literature and education – the culture brought into western
Asia by the successors of Alexander, survived to be that of
the whole eastern half of the Roman Empire; thus, to be that
of the world in which Christianity emerged, and even profoundly to influence the philosophy and science of a medieval
Islam.

This is not to say that the culture of the Roman Near East
was at all times and at all levels on a par with even the more
'popular' culture or ways of life of classical Athens. Papyri
and inscriptions, including such things as curses, inspired by
frustration and hate, written on leaden tablets, show us the
influence not only of the lofty philosophy of the Stoics, or of
Epicureans and sceptical Academics at their best, but also of
crude magic: magic, the *natural* product of pre-rational and
pre-Hellenic thought, expressed in attempts of the ignorant
and frustrated to get their way, usually in love or revenge, by
short cuts; by symbolic actions, bearing some resemblance to
what the frustrated person would like to do (e.g. maltreating a
portrait or image as a substitute for maltreating the person),
often combined with prayers to some god or power, whom it is
thought important to address by his right name. The tendency
to relieve pent-up feelings in such ways is primitive, world-

wide, and can be traced rudimentarily even in captive apes;[1] and the belief that such procedures are causally effective dies very hard. But even these magical papyri and curse-tablets are almost always written in Greek; and the theories invented from time to time to 'rationalize' such behaviour show the influence of earlier and better Greek thought as well as of Babylonian astrology. The Magi, who were unfairly credited with the invention of magic (whence the name), are probably not those of early Persia, but a section of their descendants, domiciled in the Hellenized world. They were strong in Cappadocia, where they venerated images, not only of the primitive Persian mother-goddess Anaïtis but even of 'Omanos', who is Vohumana, originally almost an abstract concept in the thought of Zoroaster: 'Good Thought', a partly personified emanation of Zoroaster's God of Truth. These western Magi were also the transmitters to the Roman world of the worship of the Persian Mithras, a cult which, adapted by and for westerners, became the personal religion of many centurions and officers of the Roman army, and appeared for a time as the most formidable rival of Christianity.

It was the international or rather de-nationalized thought of this Greco-Oriental 'middle eastern' world, with its welter of rational and irrational speculation, which issued in Gnosticism: a term describing not a single philosophy, but the theological doctrines of many thinkers, of varying degrees of profundity or shallowness. Syncretistic, or tending to a mixture of religions, and desirous to find a way of salvation or deliverance from the evils of the world, Gnosticism in the Christian era found Christianity highly congenial. Gnostics would gladly have absorbed the religion of Christ into an amalgam of all the religions and philosophies of the world, and it was only after prolonged, severe and sometimes bitter controversy that Christianity extricated itself from this dangerously friendly embrace. Christian thinkers themselves, even the orthodox, inevitably used the terms and categories of Hel-

1. Cf. my *World of Hesiod* (2nd impression Blom; New York, 1966), Ch. III.

lenistic thought when they came to philosophize about their faith. Christians as distinguished as the martyrs Justin in the second century and Cyprian in the third had been mature men, trained in the best pagan thought of their time, before they became Christians; Augustine, even later, had come under and thrown off the influence of Manicheism (the new religion of Mani of Mesopotamia, c. A.D. 259, combining Hellenized Christianity and Zoroastrianism), before his final conversion or 'commitment'. But after a struggle, the intellectual counterpart of that in which Judaism rejected militant Hellenization under the Maccabees, Christianity remained at heart comparatively matter-of-fact, earthy, practical and historically-minded, true to its Jewish ancestry.

Meanwhile mathematics, astronomy and medicine, parting company, as knowledge increased and specialization became necessary, from the general 'natural philosophy' of earlier Greece, continued to make important progress even in what might have been thought the unpromising environment of later antiquity; and it was in Ptolemy's Alexandria, in and round his great 'Museum' or Institute for Advanced Study, that much of the best work was done. Here Euclid (Eukleides), perhaps before 300 B.C., gave geometry its long-enduring system; here in the next century Aristarchos of Samos anticipated the Copernican revolution; here, Eratosthenes devised a means to measure the circumference of the earth, and Apollonios of Perga learned astronomy and mathematics from the successors of Euclid; though later, returning to his native Asia Minor, he dedicated his later books on Conics to another patron, Attalos I of Pergamon. The first century of Alexandria's history was the greatest; but original work was still being done there after five hundred years and more. Aristarchos was unable to prove his daring *hypothesis*, as he himself called it (in spite of which, Kleanthes the Stoic leader is said to have said that he ought to be prosecuted for impiety!), and the last word of the ancient world on the planetary system was that of Ptolemy the astronomer, with its arrangement of epicycles, complicated and ingenious, written out under the Antonine emperors in the second century A.D. It was the same Ptolemy who, incidentally to his astronomical work, mapped the known world as far as south-east Asia, attempting, with varying success, to define positions in terms of latitude and longitude.

Even later than Ptolemy lived two of the greatest Alexandrian mathematicians; Diophantos, who in the third century was using algebraic symbols, and (probably) Heron, who also gave accounts of mechanical contrivances using steam-power. No practical use was made of them, and this is commonly put down to a lack of interest in labour-saving devices among influential people, in a world in which hard labour was left to slaves. Yet the Roman world did introduce and use the water-mill; as the supply of slaves had long been decreasing there was, at times, a labour shortage; so perhaps the real reason for the failure to exploit the discovery of steam-power was rather that ancient metallurgy, which never produced even swords and armour nearly as good as those of the later middle ages, could not have produced high-pressure boilers that would not burst. However Heron's work remains – though we note with distress that one of the purposes for which he proposes to use steam is to fake a miracle – as evidence that even in his time applied science was not dead.

But it was the great systematizers, especially, whose names were revered in the authoritarian world which lasted for nearly 2000 years after the time of Alexander. Plato, Aristotle and Euclid were treasured, copied, annotated, expounded in thousands of lecture rooms; and with them were revered among posterity the names of Ptolemy and of a contemporary of Ptolemy, the physician and surgeon Galen of Pergamon; a man of profound learning, a practiser of dissection (though on the strength of it he seems to have reasoned too freely by analogy, from the structure of other mammalian bodies to that of man), and an immensely prolific writer. He was also a teleologist, which suited the theological bent of thought of the ensuing millennium. But if he became, as he has been called, the 'dictator of medicine' for all that time and more, it was not his fault, revealing himself, as he does, as both a first-hand observer and devoted to the free exercise of reason in argument.

When Constantine in A.D. 330 transferred the chief seat of Roman government to Byzantium and named the city after himself, it was in recognition of the superior importance of this most populous, civilized and economically prosperous eastern part of his empire, as well as of the need to keep a closer eye on Goths and Huns north of the Black Sea and lower Danube, and on Persia, once more powerful and aggressive under the Sassanid dynasty; and as capital of a mainly Greek-speaking and now a Christian Roman Empire Constantinople stood for eleven centuries, long after western and central Europe had been lost to Germanic barbarians. Not the least among the achievements of the Hellenized east was the work of the Greek Christian intellectuals or 'Doctors', Athanasios of Alexandria (not author of the famous creed called after him), Basil of Cappadocia, his brother Gregory of Nyssa and his friend Gregory of Nazianzos, and the 'golden-tongued' John Chrysostom of Antioch; all men of the Hellenized east, and all men of the fourth Christian century – which did not mean that they did not have frequent occasion to display courage in resisting the sometimes unchristian behaviour of a nominally Christian government and its officials.

For three centuries (a period little mentioned in our western history-books) the Christian emperors of Constantinople held sway over Asia Minor, Egypt and Syria as well as over the Ægean world; then, very swiftly, Egypt and Syria were lost to the immediate successors of Mohammed. Once the regular army was defeated, there was no popular resistance, and the Christian population showed little sign of wishing to return to the rule of the old empire, with its bureaucratic government, its persecuting Greek higher clergy, whose theological distinctions could scarcely even be translated into Coptic or Syriac, and its all too efficient tax-collectors. The circumstances of the loss reveal, still present even a thousand years after Alexander, what had always been the great weakness of the Hellenistic world.

For all the Hellenization of their higher culture, Egypt and Syria had never been fully assimilated, fully Hellenized. Only the Jews, through the Maccabean resistance, had succeeded in preserving their national culture and literature; elsewhere, as we have seen, writing was Greek. But speech, among the peasants and the proletariat in the towns, was not. Coptic ('Gyptic', i.e. Egyptian) survived as the language of the people, as did Semitic speech in Syria; how continuously, we may see from place-names. Under the Macedonian Seleukids, many towns had been renamed; the ancient Halep (Aleppo) became Beroia, named for Beroia in Macedonia; Hamath, Epiphaneia, after Antichos Epiphanes (but St Jerome knew that the people still called it Hamath in his time); Rabbah of Ammon, Philadelphia; but today all these and many other Greek names have perished or have to be sought in ancient sources, and the cities have returned long since to their vernacular names, as Halep, Hamah, Amman. There is some evidence even from church history that the peoples were restive under a Greek, upper-class, church government as well as secular rule; for it was these lands which most clung to theological, especially Christological doctrines, which the great Councils held at the capital or near it (Nicea, Chalcedon) had ruled out as heretical; resenting, it seems, that they should have imposed on them the subtleties of the Greeks. Most of their descendants went over, gradually, to the simplicities of Islam; but from the first, one of the attractions of Muslim rule was that not only did it, by command of the Prophet, never force Islam upon Jews or Christians, but also it was unconcerned as to whether particular Christians were heretical or orthodox.

In Asia Minor, Hellenization had been more intensive. Here Greek did in the end replace the vernaculars, though some rustic Galatians still spoke Keltic in A.D. 400. Here the Byzantine or Christian-Hellenistic 'Roman Empire', though more than once hard pressed, lasted on, and had the main source of its military strength, until late in the 11th century, with the coming of the Turks from central Asia. Armenia, with its own language and literature, though Christian, did indeed cherish its own ideological, that is inevitably theological, differences; but from Cappadocia westward we hear of no important heresies, unless we count the Iconoclastic ('image-smashing') movement in the 8th–9th centuries, a movement, strongest among the frontiersmen toughened in fighting the infidel, to 'save' the western townsmen from idolatrous practices. The Empire never appeared stronger or more stable than about A.D. 1000, when it had even recaptured north Syria, Cyprus and Crete; but the Turks caught it at a time of disputed succession, and when oppressive taxation and the greed of landlords had destroyed the economic basis of its Anatolian peasant soldiery. Winning the decisive Battle of Manzikert in 1071, the Turks occupied the central plateau and deprived the Empire for ever of its best recruiting-ground; but even then, the final end was not for nearly 400 years more, and the Empire might have lasted longer yet had it not been stabbed in the back by the aggressive and predatory west, as the Seleukids had been by Rome long before; this time, by Norman-French crusaders, intent on carving out lordships for themselves under the ideological banner of religion, who sacked Constantinople and broke up the Empire for a time, in 1204.

The ultimate heir to all the lands once unified by Persia and Hellenized, some more and some less, under the successors of Alexander, was therefore Islam; but the mission of Greece was not exhausted even with the Mohammedan conquest. The Muslim world was profoundly indebted, especially in its earlier centuries, to its Hellenized subjects, for the beginnings of its architecture, and for its higher learning in medicine, astronomy, mathematics and philosophy. The title *Almagest*, by which we still know the great work of Ptolemy, consists of the Arabic article prefixed to the Greek *megistos*, 'greatest'; algebra is *Al-gebir*, 'the greater' branch of mathematics; and if Arab mathematicians developed this, there is more than a bare beginning of it in Greek Alexandria, especially in the work of Diophantos. Aflatun and Aristu, which are the Arabic names of Plato and Aristotle, were honoured no

less in the Mohammedan world than in Europe, and gave
Muslim philosophy its starting point. It was from the Arabs,
in Spain, that the west derived its first knowledge of Aristo-
telian logic, long before the recovery of Greek in fifteenth-cen-
tury Italy, just in time, from the failing hands of Byzance. So, by
the time that the Muslim civilization itself had fallen into stag-
nation and decay, a Europe equipped once more with the legacy
of Greece, or at least considerable fragments of it, was in a position to carry on the mental exploration of the universe where
the Greeks had left it.

It remains, in a biography of Alexander, to consider the
extent of his personal contribution, as the Greek conqueror
of the 'middle east', to its subsequent history.

15 Alexander in World History

No soldier in history is more indisputably 'great' than Alexander, surpassing the majority even of good and eminent generals, as do Napoleon and very few others. What marks him out – even more than the quality both of his swift tactical insight and deliberate strategic planning – is the 'daemonic' strength of will and leadership with which he dragged a war-weary army with unbroken success to Khodjend and the Punjab. He wrote his name across the Near and Middle East for two hundred years; and yet his work was ephemeral, in that the Empire which he left, even in the strong hands of the early Seleukids, was dying on its feet from the first generation.

Even his personality *made no permanent impression* beyond the Greco-Roman world; for, as is not generally realized, the Legend of Alexander that so deeply impressed not only medieval Europe, but the world of Islam, and even lands which the historical Alexander never saw, is *not* a spontaneous growth of the age immediately after him. The versions of the *Romance of Alexander*, which existed by the fifth century A.D. in Syriac and Armenian as well as Greek and Latin – which caught the imagination of Firdausi and of Arabic poets, which penetrated even to Ethiopia, and were brought west again by the Crusaders with their incrustations of Eastern marvels – are all derived from one book, a literary forgery, ascribed to Kallisthenes, and written probably at Alexandria in the second century A.D. It became very popular in the later Empire, quite outshining the more sober and 'highbrow' popularization of Curtius.

'But this book was itself a farrago of heterogeneous elements

– pieces of genuine history, ancient stories once told in Babylon of Gilgamesh or Etanna, literary forgeries of the days soon after Alexander ... variations due to Egyptian patriotic sentiment, like that which made Alexander the son of the last Pharaoh, Nectanebus ... In the Persian version Alexander became a son of Darius; among the Mahommedans he turned into a prophet, hot against idols; the pen of Christian monks made him an ascetic saint.

'That the East today has so much to tell about Alexander is only due to the fact that old mythical stories of gods or heroes who go wandering through lands of monsters and darkness, of magic fountains and unearthly oceans, became attached to his name in the popular literature of the Roman Empire.'[1]

When the pseudo-Kallisthenes was writing, Alexander was only remembered in fiercely patriotic Sassanid Iran as the 'accursed' destroyer of the sacred books. It is characteristic of the growth of legend that the name of 'the great Secunder' in modern India attaches to cities like Secundra on the lower Jumna and Secunderabad in the Deccan, in longitudes where Alexander believed there was only the outer sea.

To return to history :

The figure of Alexander raises with exceptional clearness that fascinating and even practically important question : How far do the greatest and most successful men of action change the history of their time and after?

To discuss this question involves a certain amount of specu- lation on the might-have-been, which the most austere type of historian might condemn as unprofitable. With this austerity I cannot agree, for the reason that history should be studied not only for our entertainment or even our moral edification, but also, in Thucydides' words, as a guide to 'that future which, *in accordance with the workings of human nature*, is likely to resemble' the past. Since the experiences of history are not laboratory experiments which can be repeated with variations at will, it is genuinely important to consider what might have happened at the great crises of history – as soberly as may be,

1. Margaret Bryant in *Ency. Brit.* 11th edn, I, p. 550.

and relying always, so far as possible, on facts that *did* exist or events that *did* take place, irrespective of the historical decision of the career of the historical hero under discussion.

For greater precision the question, as regards Alexander, may well be divided into three :

How much did Alexander's triumphs owe to the circumstances of his time?

How much difference would it have made if Alexander had been killed at the outset of his career?

How much difference would it have made if Alexander had lived thirty years longer, and left an able son behind him?

It has long been a commonplace that Alexander owed to his father a better 'start' than any other conqueror in history, inheriting as he did the best army ever yet seen. We have emphasized, too, what has not been so often repeated – that the conquest of Persia had been dreamed of before him, not only by theorists, but by men of action like Jason of Pherai, who hoped to accomplish it; and also that foreign conquest formed an obvious exit from an economic impasse in Greece.

Our first question has another facet : What might a man of Alexander's gifts have done under other circumstances? – the answer to which is more purely speculative; but to the present writer's mind it is clear that in any society a man of his physical (including cerebral) make-up would have excelled in whatever road to acknowledged excellence was laid before him in youth. In a peaceful age he could have been a famous man of peace; a politician or capitalist – and probably also a notable athlete. He had also the 'insatiable curiosity' and the untiring persistence of a scientist or an explorer. And with the restraint and moderation, the touch even of puritanism shown in him, in an environment that gave him every temptation to excess and sensuality, it is clear that, born a few centuries later, he could have been a famous and dominating saint.

As to what may happen to the most brilliant soldiers if the stars are less kind, one may see it in the careers of Hannibal or of R. E. Lee. Of British commanders, the one who most resembles Alexander in far-sighted strategy, in swiftness of improvisation, and in the personal magnetism and leadership that could do so much with so little, is perhaps not any of the great victors – not Marlborough, nor Nelson, nor any of the great galaxy now living – but Montrose. To read Montrose's campaigns is to find oneself before one who had an amazing share of the 'Alexander touch'; yet he could save nothing. (Could *Alexander* have prevented Montrose's Highlanders from going home between-whiles?) While Alexander was borne on the flood, Montrose found his duty, as he saw it, call him to swim against the ebb-tide; found himself in an environment where *tout lasse, tout casse, tout passe*; and so achieved nothing except a heroic story.

But if Alexander was borne on the flood-tide, did his own personality count for nothing?

Far from it, I believe. (Many swimmers may be borne on on the same flood, but that does not prevent one from being a stronger swimmer than another.) We see Alexander faced with a *personal* choice in Syria after Issos, when Dareios offered to cede the western provinces. Parmenion was for accepting and, especially in view of the feeling in the army, surely many an invader (Philip, for instance?) would have accepted the Euphrates line, or (perhaps best) have granted a beaten Persia a frontier at the mountains east of the Tigris, after temporarily occupying her capitals. That would have been quite enough for the Greek world to digest.

Another personality played its part, too, in the weakness of Dareios. Gaugamêla seems to have been won by minutes, before Mazaios' flank attack brought the phalanx to a standstill. As it was, its centre split open and was ridden through. Suppose that Dareios had had the courage of a Pôros, or the genius for cavalry raiding of a Spitamenes . . .

Apart from Alexander's tremendous drive and ambition, his death at the outset (Kleitos saved him by half a second at the Granikos!) might, of course, have been followed by disturbances in Macedonia that would – like the assassination of Jason – have suspended the campaign indefinitely. It remains nevertheless *probable* that someone (Alexander of Lynkestis?) would have led Philip's army to the assault sooner or later – but would he have gone so far as the son of Philip?

Lastly, would it have altered the 'shape of things' out of recognition if Alexander had lived thirty years longer and left a son of the calibre that might have been expected of him?

(Here one must first remark that to suppose Alexander living even to be fifty – when Roxâne's son would have been eighteen – is a much more unlikely hypothesis, in view of his habits, than to suppose him to have died sooner.)

But, if he had lived longer, and conquered Carthage (at this time a less formidable proposition than Iran, to judge by Agathokles the Syracusan's campaigns) and perhaps even Italy (where Rome was still no more than strong enough to beat the Samnites) and pressed on with his plans to amalgamate Macedonians and Iranians, and used suitable Italians as officers, as he used Thracians or Greeks – is it likely that he could have anticipated Rome and unified the Middle East and Mediterranean world in a lasting commonwealth?

This is, of course, an immense question, involving far too many unknown quantities to admit to dogmatism. But personally, I do not think so. I do not think so, for the reasons, first, that regional feeling, in the Greek cities, in Macedonia, in Iran, in Italy and elsewhere was everywhere strong; there would in any case, surely, have been an overwhelming reaction, as soon as the strong hand was removed, against Alexander's 'godlike' internationalism; and secondly, that *there were not enough Macedonians and Greeks* to crush local particularism with ruthless brutality, as Rome was able to do. The causes that led to the crumbling of the Seleukid Empire would surely have operated as remorsely in a larger one. In a later age the Caliphate, an Empire as swiftly won, fell apart as swiftly – in spite of having one God, one Book, one Prophet, to hold it together.

Moreover, even the Greek world was not united. For all Alexander's blandishment of Athens, for all his severity to Thebes, still Athens, Sparta, Aitolia remained surly. Plenty of the landless and the uprooted were prepared to follow Alexander's fortunes; but the governments and dominant classes of the chief Greek states still held freedom – at the city level – to be more precious than Empire.

Rome had two advantages. First, the city-states and federations of villages in Italy, just because they were less brilliant than those of Greece, inspired a less fanatical *erôs* (Perikles' word for patriotism) and amalgamated more easily; while Rome herself extended her citizenship liberally to other communities. Athens had done as much for Samos and Plataia, but there are few similar cases. And second, when Rome had unified central and southern Italy – just in time for the raid of Hannibal's 26,000 men, which nearly brought her to her knees – she had unified the manpower of a larger, deeper-soiled, more populous peninsula. Her census gave her confederacy 770,000 fighting men. Macedonia's native home-levy was never as much as 50,000, and there were limits to the extent to which one could dilute with foreigners. There were probably not so many adult male Greeks in all the world; and they were scattered from the Punjab to Spain.

What difference, then, did Alexander's personality make to world history?

Clearly, he brought Greek culture – which was already penetrating the East, with its trade, its doctors, its mercenaries – into the East in a flood, and with the prestige of conquest. The Iranian and later the Arabic East reacted at last; but they had learned, at least in Syria, that the Greeks 'had something', and here, too, under Islam, captive Greece led her captivity captive.

But, whereas it seems almost certain that the west of the Persian Empire, as it was in the fourth century, must have fallen away into the Mediterranean orbit – it was Alexander and no one else who insisted on leading Greek arms to Bactria and India. Few other men would have tried, let alone succeeded.

Was this in its effect for the good of the world?

I cannot think so.

By marching into Iran, Alexander overstepped the bounds of the Mediterranean world; and it was his *personal* achievement, by conquering so much, to lay a greater strain than could be borne upon the strength of the Seleukid Empire – his residuary legatee.

Moreover, by drawing off so much Greek manpower so far into the East, Alexander weakened Greek colonization nearer home, and ultimately even Greek resistance at home to Roman aggression.

To urge that Alexander 'ought to' have turned west earlier is idle; as idle as to condemn him on moral grounds under the Actonian aphorism 'Absolute power corrupts absolutely. Every great man is a bad man'; as idle as to condemn, with the brilliant French historian, M. Léon Homo, the 'error' of the Roman Republic in turning east after him. The East offered 'glittering prizes' and, because it consciously tried to defend itself, *looked* threatening. The West, really more dangerous, offered no attraction; it was still mostly primeval forest. To blame Alexander for his appalling record of butchery, his career of piracy on the grand scale (as a captured pirate is said once to have pointed out to him), is to blame him for not being brought up a Christian or a Greek republican.

But there were conscious Greek efforts, especially under Alexander of Epeiros and under Pyrrhos, to check the Western danger, already threatening the Greeks of Italy; and if the Greek drive to the East had not happened to find a leader of such transcendent brilliance, and therefore to penetrate so far, the Greek offensive and defensive in the West *would* have had more weight behind it. What a blessing to humanity if the Greeks could have checked Rome, at least long enough to civilize her, before Italy became the centre of a unified Mediterranean world. The Romans took kindly enough to Greek art and thought in the end; but they (far more than any other barbarians) *first* broke the back of Greek civilization, in the appalling last two centuries B.C. before, with Vergil and Augustus, they learned to spare as well as conquer.

To sum up:

With all allowance for the tendencies of his age, the powerful personality of Alexander did make a difference; but the difference he made consisted in carrying much farther the

Greek push into nearer Asia, which would almost certainly
have taken place even without him; and the effect of this was
to overstrain the strength of Hellenism (very much as Napoleon overstrained the strength of France) with results that were
not ultimately for the good of humanity.

Perhaps, after all, the world is wrong in finding so much
difference between the failure of a Montrose and the success
of an Alexander.

Notes on Books

The following books may be recommended to the general reader, and do not presuppose a knowledge of Greek or Latin.

Original Sources

Arrian, *The Campaigns of Alexander* (*Anabasis Alexandrou*) has been translated in the old *Bohn's Classical Library*, in the *Loeb Library* and in the *Penguin Classics* (best read in 2nd edition, with introduction by J. R. Hamilton).

Plutarch, *Life of Alexander*, exists in many English translations, from North's (a fine piece of Elizabethan prose, but made via a French translation and not always accurate) to the *Loeb Library* (see above). This, the most read book on Alexander, is unfortunately not one of Plutarch's best lives; he makes one or two quite obvious errors, and the letters of Alexander, or to him, which he uses extensively, were at least in many cases literary forgeries, produced soon after Alexander's death. The Roman Q. Curtius' *History of Alexander* (Loeb), a 'popular' work of its day, is rhetorical and tiresome, but uses, among sources hostile to A., one which drew, very interestingly, upon the reminiscences of one of Dareios' Greek mercenaries, perhaps their commander Patron (pp. 125–6).

Modern Writers on Alexander

Historians writing before about 1920 usually, while not blind to Alexander's greatness, adopt a critical attitude towards him, while those from *c.* 1920 to 1950 are often very adoring : a fact perhaps not without social significance. Some of the best are :

Grote, *History of Greece*, Vol. XII (1856); reprinted in Everyman's Library (Dent).

D. G. Hogarth, *Philip and Alexander of Macedon* (John Murray, 1897).

B. I. Wheeler, *Alexander the Great*, in the *Heroes of the Nations* series (Putnam, New York and London, 1900).

F. A. Wright, *Alexander the Great* (Routledge, 1934); very readable, but regards Alexander as almost above criticism.

U. Wilcken, *Alexander der Grosse* (Leipzig, 1931; English translation, Chatto & Windus, 1932), is marked by strong common sense, and is perhaps the best recent biography.

W. W. Tarn's chapters in *Cambridge Ancient History*, Vol. VI, are reprinted as Vol. I of his *Alexander the Great*; see below.

Major-General J. F. C. Fuller's *The Generalship of Alexander the Great* (Eyre and Spottiswoode, 1958) is good on its subject.

On Alexander in Afghanistan, and India in Alexander's time, see also: Sir Aurel Stein, *On Alexander's Track to the Indus* (London, 1928); Tarn, *The Greeks in Bactria and India* (Cambridge University Press, 2nd edition, 1956.)

P. Jouguet, *L'Impérialisme macédonien et l'Hellénisation de l'Orient* (Paris, La Renaissance du Livre, 1926; English translation in *History of Civilization* series, Kegan Paul, 1928), covers in about 400 pages both the career of Alexander and the Hellenistic Age.

W. W. Tarn, *Alexander the Great* (Vol. I, *The Narrative*; Vol. II, *Sources and Studies*, Cambridge, 1948), is the most influential work on Alexander which has appeared in Britain during this century; though too favourable to its hero, in the present writer's opinion (see my review, in *Journal of Hellenic Studies*, Vol. 67); see also E. Badian in *Classical Quarterly*, 1958, and other articles.

P. Green, *Alexander the Great* (Weidenfeld & Nicolson 1971) is sensational, and has been editorially cut to make room for the pictures, but is well researched.

The Hellenistic Age

For the world after Alexander, see Tarn's and Rostovtzeff's chapters in the *Cambridge Ancient History*, Vols. VI and VII.

Other standard works are:

W. W. Tarn, *Antigonos Gonatas* (Oxford U.P., 1913).

W. W. Tarn and G. T. Griffith, *Hellenistic Civilisation* (Arnold, 3rd edition, 1952).

M. Cary, Vol. III of Methuen's *History of the Greek and Roman World*.

W. S. Ferguson, *Hellenistic Athens* (Macmillan, 1911).

E. R. Bevan, *The House of Seleucus* (Arnold, 1902).

E. R. Bevan and J. P. Mahaffy, *Egypt under the Ptolemaic Dynasty* (Methuen, 1927).

Bury, Bevan, Barber and Tarn, *The Hellenistic Age* (Cambridge U.P., 1925) is perhaps still the best introduction to the subject, for those who know something about classical Greece; four lectures by high authorities: 150 pages.

For Greek culture in the Roman and early Christian Near East, see chapters in *Cambridge Ancient History*, Vols. XI, XII, and *Cambridge Mediaeval History*, Vol. I; and especially the invaluable work of Sir Ernest Barker, *From Alexander to Constantine*.

E. R. Bevan's *Alexander in Ency. Brit.*, 1911, is an excellent brief study, unhappily replaced in the latest edition by the work of an amateur disciple of Tarn.

For the continuing argument on A.'s work and character, see now: *Alexander the Great: the Main Problems* (a collection of articles by several scholars) ed. G. T. Griffith (Heffer, Cambridge, 1965); and, at a more 'popular' level, the articles in a special number of *Greece and Rome* devoted to him (Oxford U.P., 1965).

Index